BASIC INTRODUCTION
TO THE NEW TESTAMENT

JOHN STOTT

BASIC INTRODUCTION
TO THE
NEW TESTAMENT

revised by

Stephen Motyer

WILLIAM B. EERDMANS PUBLISHING COMPANY

GRAND RAPIDS, MICHIGAN

Wm. B. Eerdmans Publishing Co.
2140 Oak Industrial Drive, N.E., Grand Rapids, Michigan 49505
www.eerdmans.com

Printed in the United States of America

23 22 21 20 19 18 17   1 2 3 4 5 6 7

ISBN 978-0-8028-7469-6

Library of Congress Cataloguing-in-Publication Data

Names: Stott, John R. W., author. | Motyer, Stephen, 1950–   reviser.
Title: Basic introduction to the New Testament / John Stott ; revised by   Stephen
    Motyer.
Other titles: Men with a message
Description: Grand Rapids : Eerdmans Publishing Co., 2017. | Includes index.
    | "Text Copyright © 1951 by John R. W. Stott, originally published under the
    title Men with a Message. Previously published by Eerdmans © 1964 under
    the title Basic Introduction to the New Testament. ISBN 0802811906. Revised
    edition published by Baker Books © 2001 under the title The Story of the New
    Testament: Men with a Message."
Identifiers: LCCN 2016037625 | ISBN 9780802874696 (pbk. : alk. paper)
Subjects: LCSH: Bible. New Testament—Introductions.
Classification: LCC BS2330.3 .S76 2017 | DDC 225.6/1—dc23
    LC record available at https://lccn.loc.gov/2016037625

Contents

Foreword

O ne of London's ancient streets is called Threadneedle Street. To stand there is to find ourselves at the center of Roman London. The street derives its name from the Merchant Taylors Company located in that area since the sixteenth century. Although All Souls Langham Place, where John Stott was the minister, is not in that immediate vicinity, I still associate Threadneedle Street with him.

And here is the reason: because of his unique ability to thread the needle through a passage of scripture, or a book of the Bible, without tearing the text or pulling it out of shape. It is no surprise that, while still in the infancy of his ministry, he was invited by the Bishop of London to write a book that would encourage the serious study of the Bible.

The largest part of the content of this book has been around for as long as Her Majesty Queen Elizabeth has been on the throne. (She became queen in 1952 and her Coronation was June 2, 1953.) Part of John Stott's role as chaplain to the queen was in helping her fulfil her promise to "maintain the Laws of God and the true profession of the Gospel." It intrigues me to think of the possibility of her having a copy of this book in her library!

The first copyright is dated 1951. My earliest copy was purchased in 1962 from the bookstall at the Keswick Convention. The dates are important, testifying as they do to the way in which this book continues to stand the test of time.

The bold, clean cover of this trim new edition certainly catches the eye, but it is the compelling relevance of the content that has kept it in print for so long, and which will continue to serve generations who never enjoyed the privilege of hearing John Stott preach. It is surely a mark of Stott's humility that he saw how his earlier work could be improved upon with the help of another. It is equally a mark of Stephen Motyer's ability that he accepted the invitation to update the content. Their shared vision to enable Christians to love, understand, and obey the Bible has resulted in this easily readable and wonderfully helpful book.

Many members of our congregations (more than we like to admit), despite attending Bible-teaching churches, have difficulty understanding and explaining the big picture. This brief introduction will be a terrific help, not just for them, but also for those of us who teach. Confusion in the pew must at least in part be due to a lack of clarity in the pulpit. This book has helped me to understand more about the men God used and the message they proclaimed. And so as an unashamed "fan" of this work, I commend it to you with the prayer that a whole new generation will be helped to understand the message properly, to live it out faithfully, and to proclaim it boldly.

ALISTAIR BEGG, *Senior Minister*
Parkside Church, Chagrin Falls, Ohio

Preface

It was soon after my institution in 1950 as Rector of All Souls Langham Place that, to my utter astonishment, Bishop William Wand (who had both ordained and instituted me) invited me to write for 1954 what was known as "the Bishop of London's Lent Book." The result was *Men with a Message.* It was in fact my first book, two years before *Fundamentalism and Evangelism,* and four years before *Basic Christianity* and *What Christ Thinks of the Church.*

In the early 1950s I was reading and thinking a good deal about the inspiration of Scripture, and about the relations between its divine and human authors. I was specially impressed by the need to emphasize that the particularity of each New Testament author was in no way smothered by the unique process of inspiration. On the contrary, as I wrote in the 1954 introduction to the book, "the Holy Spirit first prepared, and then used, their individuality of upbringing, experience, temperament and personality, in order to convey through each some distinctive and appropriate truth." So this became, and remains, the underlying theme of *Basic Introduction to the New Testament.*

I firmly believe that the book's revised contents and new look will make it a lot more readable than its rather stodgy and compressed first edition!

Easter, 1994

Editor's Note

Stephen Motyer's revision of this book, made at John Stott's invitation, aimed to make its content accessible to further generations by lightening the language and relating it to more recent biblical scholarship. Professor Motyer retained the structure of the original chapters but rewrote them in a more contemporary style. He also added chapters on Mark and Matthew, which were left out of the original 1954 version.

Each chapter examines the authorship of a particular New Testament book or books and thereby provides a brief introduction to the context and content of each book, as well. One of the chief purposes of this book is to explore the variety of these authors. They were individuals with diverse backgrounds, personalities, and experiences, and their writings reflect this diversity.

In the case of the Gospels, for instance, it seems that the evangelists deliberately set out to supplement each other in the light of their individual purposes and concerns. Thus Matthew greatly expanded Mark; Luke introduced new emphases into material drawn from the other two, and added yet more; and John painted a portrait of Jesus which went beyond all three, both in content and in spiritual depth. And so for each of the New Testament writers. They were all chosen by God, shaped by experience, and empowered by the Spirit, first to understand the revolutionary Good News of Jesus, and then to communicate and apply it in the various situations they faced.

But at the same time they did not proclaim many messages. In the midst of their variety, they communicate one message of the saving grace of God in Christ. The "gospel" may be expressed in different words and applied to different needs, but incorporates one message for all men and women in all times and places. In this book it is the variety which is chiefly stressed, but through it hopefully the unity will also emerge:

- the unified awareness of the world's need, estranged from God and afflicted by sin
- the unified belief in the initiative of God, who has taken action to deliver the world from evil and to reconcile it with himself
- the unified focus of this initiative on Jesus Christ, who has been anointed and appointed by God to be the world's Savior
- the unified belief in the engagement of God, who does not just act *through* Jesus, but acts personally *in* him
- the unified belief in the exaltation of Jesus Christ, who dies and rises again so that we might share the life of God himself.

These elements are all there in the writings of all the New Testament authors, differently expressed but equally fundamental. Only in one case is something missing: the little letter of James contains no reference to the death of Christ as the focus of his saving identification with us. But that belief is not incompatible with James' "message." Did he reject it? Certainly not. He could never have led the church in Jerusalem for so long if he did. His letter was bound by its immediate concerns, and these were met without any reference to the cross.

Readers will notice that the very brief letter of Jude (only twenty-five verses) has not been included here. Since the book devotes a full chapter to each writer and has only one chapter each on Paul and Luke, who together were responsible for half of the New Testament, a complete chapter on such a short letter would not be a good balance.

This reissue of *Basic Introduction to the New Testament* takes the very best that John Stott and Stephen Motyer have to offer, while presenting it in a trim, straightforward, paperback version. Along with Professor Motyer and the late John Stott, the Wm. B. Eerdmans Publishing Co. hopes that this book will continue to provide evangelical believers with what Professor Motyer has called "a first-rate introduction to the New Testament."

CHAPTER 1

Mark and His Message

Then he called the crowd to him along with his disciples and said: "If anyone would come after me, he must deny himself and take up his cross and follow me."

(Mark 8:34)

Mark's is the Gospel for disciples. He shares with the other evangelists the concern to enable his readers to understand the person of "Jesus Christ, the Son of God" (1:1). But he goes further than merely presenting Jesus. Jesus is the principal character in Mark's drama, but the disciples come a close second.

Throughout the story, Mark is concerned with discipleship—its privileges, hindrances, dangers, challenges, and perplexities. This is the distinctive emphasis of Mark's Gospel. In a very human and encouraging way he reveals how difficult it was for Jesus' first followers to take their initial steps in discipleship, and how patiently Jesus persevered with them even though their understanding was so limited and their obedience so fragile. As we shall see, this emphasis probably grew out of Mark's own experience as a Christian.

A Ground-Breaking Production

Mark's Gospel was probably the first of the four to be written, and thus broke new ground and paved the way for the others to follow his pattern. His contribution was enormous, for nothing quite like this had ever been written before. In several striking respects, Mark's record of Jesus differs from other ancient biographies of the famous:

- Mark announces at the start that his subject is no mere man but "the Son of God."
- He classifies his work with a new name: it is a "Gospel" (1:1).
- He tells nothing about the birth or childhood of his subject.
- He records surprisingly little of Christ's teaching, though frequently mentions that he taught (e.g. 1:38f.; 2:2).
- He devotes about a third of his book to recounting the death of his subject.
- His work is surprisingly short! Did he really have no more than these sixteen short chapters to say about this "Son of God"?
- Why does he spend so much of this brief space focusing attention, not on his chief subject, but on the disciples who gathered around him?

All these features make Mark's record of Jesus unique among biographies of the time. The other evangelists make up some of these omissions. Both Matthew and Luke actually reproduce most of the content of Mark's Gospel in their own, combining it with additional material, particularly adding birth-stories and longer records of Jesus' teaching. As a result, they are both considerably longer—in Luke's case, almost twice as long. But they do not help us to understand why Mark paved the way with such an extraordinary work.

The answers to some of these questions may lie in the experience of Mark himself. Who was he?

Mark the Man

Like the other evangelists, Mark was not anxious to advertise his own identity in his Gospel. He does not mention himself by name. But others were keen to record the name of its author, and "According to Mark" was attached to it from the earliest years. If there had been widespread doubt about the ascription, tradition would undoubtedly have fixed on a figure of greater prominence in the early church. So we can be confident that this book was written by a "Mark." Fortunately we can identify him with ease, and the New Testament evidence allows us to paint a fascinating portrait of him.

1. Mark belonged to a founding family of the Christian church

Undoubtedly he is the "John, also called Mark" mentioned in Acts 12:12 and 25. He is not unusual in having two names reflecting a bilingual background, and in his case the fact that one of them is Latin (Mark) may point to family connections with the Roman forces in Palestine. Mark's Latin background is indicated also by the presence of some Latin words in his Gospel.

In Acts 12 we find the church gathered in the house of Mark's mother, Mary, to pray for Peter in prison. This house was obviously an important center in the life of the early Jerusalem church, for Peter went straight there when he was miraculously released, obviously assuming that he would find the church there. It must have been a large house, and Mark's family was wealthy enough to afford at least one servant-girl, the excitable Rhoda, who left Peter on the doorstep. Some scholars have speculated that this house contained the famous "large upper room" in which the Last Supper was held (Mark 14:15), and in which the church gathered after Jesus' ascension (Acts 1:13).

3

2. Mark was an eyewitness of Jesus' death and resurrection

Mark may have traveled to see and hear Jesus elsewhere, but if he lived in Jerusalem then he must have witnessed the final events in Jesus' ministry. We can imagine the impact these had on the young Mark. He meditated on the meaning of Jesus' death. And when he came to write his Gospel, it became the focus of the whole story, foreshadowed as early as Mark 3:6, predicted frequently by Jesus who traveled to Jerusalem deliberately in order to die, and interpreted as a sacrificial death, a "ransom for many" (10:45). We will survey this central aspect of his message below.

It is likely that he went through a painful development similar to that which Peter underwent (see chapter 8): starting with a traditional belief in a conquering, victorious Messiah who would re-establish the Jews as the sovereign people of God, he came to see the Messiah as a suffering figure, dying for his people to save them from their sins. This was the "Christ, the Son of God" whose story was "good news" for all who would hear it (1:1).

3. Mark experienced failure in his own discipleship

This is most important for our understanding of the way in which his experience equipped Mark to write his Gospel.

Paul and Barnabas were present in Mark's home for that famous prayer meeting when Peter was released from prison. Now Barnabas was actually Mark's cousin (Colossians 4:10); and when they left to return to Antioch, he and Paul took Mark with them (Acts 12:25). Shortly after this, the Holy Spirit prompted the church in Antioch to send Paul and Barnabas out on a daring new missionary venture (Acts 13:2f.). They took Mark along as their "helper" (13:5) as they preached the gospel through Cyprus and then crossed the sea to Pamphylia in the Roman province of Galatia.

At that point, however, Mark decided not to continue, and left Paul and Barnabas in order to "return to Jerusalem" (Acts 13:13). This upset Paul deeply, for later he refused to take Mark with him again "because he had deserted them in Pamphylia and had not continued with them in the work" (Acts 15:38). The word "desert" here is the same as that used in the parable of the sower concerning the seed on stony ground: "Those on the rock are the ones who receive the word with joy when they hear it, but they have no root. They believe for a while, but in the time of testing they *fall away*" (Luke 8:13). That is how Paul thought of Mark. When facing the test, he had "fallen away" and shown himself to be a disciple without roots, unwilling to obey the Spirit's calling.

We do not know why Mark gave up. Pamphylia was a low-lying, fever-infested area, and they were facing a hard journey up into Pisidia. Mark had just witnessed an emotionally draining confrontation with Elymas the sorcerer in Paphos (Acts 13:6–12). And maybe he had some inkling of what lay ahead. If he had traveled on with Paul and Barnabas, he would have faced physical persecution at Lystra, where Paul was nearly stoned to death (Acts 14:19). It seems as though the stress and danger became too much for him to cope with, and he fled back home to Jerusalem. We can speculate that he was a rather timid, home-loving young man!

History has a way of repeating itself. Was Mark himself the young man described in Mark 14:51f., who follows Jesus to Gethsemane wearing only a coat, and then flees naked when the Sanhedrin police try to arrest him along with Jesus? Tradition has long maintained that he was. If so, it is not hard to imagine the sense of failure Mark must have felt in Pamphylia, when he found himself unable for the second time to cope with the challenge of discipleship. But we can also see how, through this experience, he was equipped to give his Gospel its distinctive message of encouragement to those who find discipleship hard. We will survey Mark's teaching about discipleship below, but it is worth noting two features of it here, because they fit so clearly with Mark's own experience:

a. Mark uniquely emphasizes the fear felt by the disciples as they follow Jesus

Matthew and Luke tone down his language, or even omit it altogether, at three points where he mentions this fear.

- In Mark 4:40f. he tells us that the disciples are "terrified" (using a very strong expression) when they see Jesus calm the storm—and very humanly makes it clear that it is not just the waves which terrify the disciples: far more than this, it is the realization of Jesus' sheer greatness and power.
- Similarly, in 10:32 he records that the disciples are "astonished" and "afraid" as they follow Jesus up to Jerusalem, even before Jesus emphasized to them yet again his coming suffering and death (10:33f.).
- And most remarkably of all, he finishes his Gospel on a note of bewilderment and fear, as he describes the reaction of the women to the announcement of the resurrection. They are asked to pass on the message that the risen Jesus will meet his disciples in Galilee. But instead, "trembling and bewildered, the women went out and fled from the tomb. They said nothing to anyone, because they were afraid" (16:8).

From the earliest years, copyists felt that this was a most inappropriate ending for the Gospel, and provided alternatives. It is certainly possible that Mark's original ending has been lost in transmission. But it is clear from the ancient Greek manuscripts of Mark that none of the alternatives provided is original. And in fact it fits with Mark's overall portrait of the human weakness of Jesus' followers that he should end his Gospel in this most striking fashion.

b. Mark uniquely emphasizes the willingness of Jesus to
   rely on disciples who are still very insecure in their faith

In Mark 6:7-13 Jesus sends out the Twelve equipped with authority to preach and heal in his name. We read that "they went out
and preached that people should repent. They drove out many
demons and anointed many sick people with oil and healed them"
(6:12f.), and then "gathered around Jesus and reported to him all
they had done and taught" (6:30). At first sight these disciples
seem like spiritual giants, but the story immediately goes on to
paint their true colors: their hearts are hardened (6:52), their
understanding is dull (7:18), and their memory is obtuse (8:2-5;
compare 6:35-38), so that Jesus has to plead with them, "Do you
still not see or understand? Are your hearts hardened? Do you
have eyes but fail to see, and ears but fail to hear? And don't you
remember?" (8:17f.).

And even when the disciples eventually decide that Jesus is
"the Christ" (8:29), they have made only a bare start. They need
to learn hard lessons about prayer (9:28f.; 11:21-25), about humility (10:13-16), about self-sacrifice (10:26-31), and about status
(9:38f.; 10:35-45). And Mark gives little indication of progress.
Peter, James and John fall asleep instead of praying in Gethsemane
(14:37-42), and when Jesus is arrested "everyone deserted him
and fled" (14:50). The one disciple who turns back and follows
Jesus then denies him vociferously (14:71).

Behind all this we may see the experience of Mark himself.
He too had experienced the conflicting impulses he portrays in
Jesus' first disciples. On the one hand they feel immensely drawn
to Jesus (1:16-20), directly experience his extraordinary powers
(6:13), identify him as "the Christ" (8:29), give up everything to
follow him (10:28), and feel ready to die for him (14:31). But on
the other hand they are constantly puzzled or amazed by Jesus,
so much so that Mark makes little distinction between them and
the Pharisees, so far as their understanding of him is concerned

(8:11–21). As we have seen, they are frequently very fearful, and finally fall away completely.

Mark thus speaks sympathetically to all who feel the sheer difficulty of following this Christ. But is he finally hopeless about the possibility of real, victorious discipleship? It is vital that we move to a fourth feature of "Mark the man" which sheds further light on his Gospel:

4. Mark became the companion both of Peter and of Paul

Failure was not the end of the story for Mark. We do not know how long he stayed in Jerusalem after returning there. But after the apostolic Council in Acts 15, we find him back in Antioch again with Barnabas and Paul. Paul refused to take Mark with them on a return visit to the same churches. But at the cost of his partnership with Paul, Barnabas graciously helped Mark back into missionary work, taking him again to Cyprus, the scene of his failure (Acts 15:38f.).

We do not hear of Mark again until we meet him in four of the later New Testament letters. At the time of writing Colossians and Philemon (some ten or twelve years later), Mark is with Paul, who even calls him "my fellow worker" (Philemon 24; compare Colossians 4:10). And then Mark receives a glowing testimonial in Paul's last letter, written probably just before his death: Paul tells Timothy to "get Mark and bring him with you, because he is helpful [or 'useful'] to me in my ministry" (2 Timothy 4:11). Obviously the breach with Paul has been completely healed!

Finally Mark appears in 1 Peter 5:13, where Peter calls him warmly "my son" as he passes on greetings from Mark, who is with him, to the Christians in "Pontus, Galatia, Cappadocia, Asia and Bithynia," to whom the letter is addressed (1 Peter 1:1).

All these letters were probably written from Rome, where clearly Mark ministered both to Peter and to Paul, and became a trusted and much loved companion of both. Clearly, too, he was by this time known to the churches in Galatia and Asia Minor, the very area from which he had fled when his faith failed. So Barnabas' care for his cousin had been amply vindicated. Mark had faced and conquered his fears, and had become thoroughly "useful" in Christian service.

And not only Mark. Peter, too, had come back from failure to be the "Rock" on which the church was being built. Mark emphasizes Peter's failure more than that of the other disciples. "Even if all fall away, I will not.... Even if I have to die with you, I will never disown you" (14:29, 31). Then, with dreadful pathos and irony, Mark tells the story of each of the three denials predicted by Jesus (14:66–72). The denials become more emphatic, until "he began to call down curses on himself, and he swore to them, 'I don't know this man you're talking about'" (14:71).

Perhaps the friendship between Peter and Mark was cemented by their shared experience of failure and restoration. Quite possibly the Gospel itself was born out of this shared experience. From an early date it was believed that Mark based his Gospel on the preaching of Peter. The earliest statement of this view comes from Papias, the Bishop of Hierapolis around AD 130. It is supported later in the second century by Irenaeus (Bishop of Lyons *c.* AD 178–195), who adds the thought that Mark wrote down his record of Peter's preaching in Rome, after the latter's death. Then Clement of Alexandria (*c.* AD 200) contributes the suggestion that Mark was pressed to do this by the people who had heard Peter preach.

We do not know the exact sequence of events. But we can say for sure that:

- Mark spent time ministering with Peter in Rome;
- Peter features more prominently than any other disciple in Mark's Gospel;
- his Gospel was written for a western, perhaps Roman, audience;

- his Gospel would have been especially appropriate and encouraging for Christians facing the challenge of persecution.

These observations have led the American scholar William Lane to take seriously the tradition that Mark based his Gospel on the substance of Peter's preaching, and to suggest that Mark wrote it especially for the church in Rome when it was called to face persecution under Nero in AD 65, during which quite possibly Peter himself was martyred.

If Mark based his Gospel on the preaching of Peter, then some of its surprising features are explained.

- *Its length:* Mark simply used the material which he had heard Peter employ. He did not undertake further research, as Luke did.
- *Its start:* Peter clearly did not use stories of Jesus' birth and childhood in his ministry. When he summarized Jesus' ministry for Cornelius, he spoke of it "beginning in Galilee after the baptism that John preached" (Acts 10:37).
- *Its name:* the name that Mark chose for his book, "Gospel," reflects its origin in the preaching of the "good news of Jesus Christ" for which Peter and the other apostles were known.
- *Its focus:* behind Mark's emphasis on the death of Jesus we can hear Peter trying to persuade Jews that Jesus really was "the Christ, the Son of God" even though he died a criminal's death. His death fulfilled Scripture!

Mark the Writer

We can tell more about Mark simply from his writing. Here, too, he displays the particular qualities and gifts which matched him to the task of being the first Gospel-writer. Three things in particular stand out.

1. Mark was a gifted stylist

He writes in a vivid, direct and racy style. The little Greek word *euthus* is a favorite of his, used forty-one times. Translated "immediately," "just then," "straightaway," "without delay," "at once," this word adds a sense of pace and movement. Mark underlines this by using short sentences and vivid, punchy vocabulary. The story moves along rapidly from incident to incident.

Mark has a gift for visual detail which brings a scene to life. Often he includes a detail which Matthew and Luke omit. For instance, only he records that Jesus "took a little child . . . in his arms" as he said, "whoever welcomes one of these little children in my name welcomes me" (Mark 9:36f.). Only he records that the rich young man "ran up" to Jesus and "fell on his knees" before asking, "What must I do to inherit eternal life?" (10:17). And only he describes how Jesus "looked at him and loved him" (10:21), and how the man's "face fell" (10:22).

Examples could be multiplied. This love of graphic detail often means that Mark's stories are fuller than their equivalents in Matthew and Luke. For instance, we may compare the statistics of the double story of Jairus' daughter and the woman with the hemorrhage:

- Mark tells it in 395 words, 5:21–43.
- Luke uses 285 words, 8:40–56.
- Matthew manages it in only 138 words, 9:18–26.

Some of the details which Mark alone includes add the "human touch" to this story:

- Jairus does not just "plead" with Jesus to come, but asks him "repeatedly" (literally "saying many things").
- The woman "had suffered a great deal under the care of many doctors" and "instead of getting better she grew worse" (5:26).

- When she touched Jesus' coat he "realized that power had gone out from him" and so "turned around in the crowd," and then "kept looking around to see who had done it" (5:30, 32).
- When Jesus arrived at Jairus' house there were "people crying and wailing loudly" (5:38).
- Jesus then "took the child's father and mother . . . with him" and "went in where the child was" (5:40).
- And then Mark adds an unusually vivid touch, something he does on three other occasions also: he retains Jesus' original Aramaic word of command, *Talitha koum!,* "Little girl, get up!" (5:41).

Another technique employed by Mark the stylist to make his narrative come alive is the so-called "historic present." This is the sudden use of the present tense in a story set in the past. In the story of Jairus and his daughter, this happens when Jairus appears: he *"comes"* and seeing Jesus *"falls* at his feet and *urges* him" to come. Similarly Mark uses the present tense at the climax of the story. When Jesus arrives at Jairus' house, he *"sees* a commotion," *"speaks"* to the mourners, *"goes in"* with the parents, and *"says"* to the girl . . . .

Altogether Mark is a powerful stylist.

2. *Mark was a compelling story-teller*

This is the complementary quality on a larger scale. Just as Mark tells his individual stories with great vividness and power, so he composes his whole Gospel with equal skill.

The early Christian writer Papias certainly got this wrong. In the passage where he testifies that Mark based his Gospel on Peter's preaching, Papias also says that Mark "wrote down accurately whatever he remembered of the things said or done by the Lord, but not however in order." This lack of "order" he attributes to Peter, who did not draw up "a connected account of the Lord's oracles." So Mark copied Peter, simply aiming not to leave anything out.

But Mark's Gospel is anything but a jumble of disconnected reminiscences. Recently scholars have come to appreciate Mark's story more clearly than ever. It is beautifully composed, and its riches are still being explored. Through such careful composition, Mark lent force to the message he sought to communicate. Here just a few features can be mentioned:

a. Overall structure

After the introduction in 1:1–15, the Gospel clearly falls into two parts, with 8:27–30 forming the "hinge" in the middle. Peter's confession of Jesus as "the Christ" is the climax of the narrative so far. But it introduces a dramatic change: "He then began to teach them that the Son of Man must suffer many things and be rejected . . . and that he must be killed" (8:31). This note of coming suffering has been part of the story before, but not predicted by Jesus. Now the cross begins to loom large, as we will see below.

On either side of this "hinge," each half falls into three sections. In the first half, each of these sections begins with a story about the disciples (1:16–20, 3:13–19, 6:6–13), and ends with a little summary incident that encapsulates the message of that section:

- 3:7–12: great crowds are attracted to Jesus, who heals and teaches them. The demons know who he is (compare 1:1).
- 6:1–6: in contrast to 3:7–12, Jesus' home town rejects him, and he can do no healings there. The note of conflict and opposition runs right through this section.
- 8:22–26: this two-stage healing (only in Mark) illustrates what needs to happen to the disciples. Throughout this section, they have been struggling to understand Jesus. They see what

he does, but they do not comprehend it, like the man who sees people looking like walking trees (8:24). Jesus restores his comprehension, and immediately Peter's confession follows: "You are the Christ" (8:29).

The second half of the Gospel likewise falls into three sections: 8:31–10:52 (ending with the healing of a blind man, like the section it follows); 11:1–13:37 (focusing on opposition and conflict, like the middle section of the first half); and 14:1–16:8 (which tells the story of the death of Jesus, reaching a climax with the centurion's confession, which takes us right back to the beginning, 1:1, 11).

b. Repetition and reminiscence

Frequently Mark makes the narrative repeat itself, and these repetitions are vital to his message.

- On a large scale, we notice the three vital occasions on which Jesus is identified as "the Son of God" in connection with a direct word from heaven itself: in 1:10f. at his baptism, in 9:7 at the transfiguration, and in 15:39 by the centurion following the "tearing" of the Temple veil "from top to bottom" (here the veil is "torn" as heaven is "torn" in 1:10—Mark uses the same word). Divine testimony is followed by human testimony: will the readers add their voices to that of the centurion?
- On a smaller scale, there are repeated miraculous feedings (6:30–44; 8:1–10), repeated healings of the blind (7:31–37; 8:22–26; 10:46–52), repeated miraculous calmings of stormy water (4:35–41; 6:47–52), and repeated exorcisms (all very different: 1:21–28; 5:1–20; 7:24–30; 9:14–29). In all these cases the later instances remind us of the earlier ones, and the differences point up different facets of Jesus' ministry, or different challenges faced by the disciples, or by Mark's readers.

- On a smaller scale still, Mark creates subtle connections between stories which highlight aspects of his message. For instance, he creates a most surprising comparison between the poor demon-possessed boy in chapter 9, and the other young man (rich, religious, well-educated) whom Jesus meets in chapter 10. Both of them have been something "from childhood"—the one demon-possessed, the other obedient to the commandments (9:21; 10:20). But both are equally trapped, the one by the evil spirit, the other by his wealth; both can only be delivered by the direct power of God (9:29; 10:27); in both cases the disciples realize their own inability to do anything (9:28; 10:26).

But one is delivered, the other not. And what makes the difference between them is the faith *and prayer* of the father: "I do believe; help me overcome my unbelief!" (9:24).

c. Creative juxtapositions

The connection between these two "boys" in adjacent chapters is also an illustration of "creative juxtaposition." Mark combines stories, or tells them alongside each other, without making any explicit comment, but allowing them to interpret each other.

One example is the combination of the cleansing of the Temple and the cursing of the fig tree in 11:11–25. Mark tells the stories together, wrapping one story around the other—a technique he employs also in 5:21–43 and 6:7–31. Each story fills out the message of the other. The "fig tree" was one of several trees which were often used as an image for Israel. Inspecting the Temple in 11:11 is followed by examining the fig tree in 11:12–14—and cursing it as fruitless. Then the cursing is followed by what we usually call the "cleansing" of the Temple, though it is more like an act of judgment. The one whose "house" it is (11:17) has examined it and found it wanting.

The next day the disciples notice that the fig tree has withered. An ominous sign! And then Jesus gives them radical new teaching on prayer which completely bypasses the Temple, the "house of prayer for all nations" (11:22–25). We are not at all surprised when, later that day, Jesus predicts the total destruction of the Temple (13:2).

No parts of this combined story would have the same meaning if the other parts were not there. Examples of this technique could be multiplied from other parts of Mark's Gospel.

3. Mark was a persuasive spokesman

The purpose of all this careful writing was to persuade. Whom did Mark have in mind? Scholars are not agreed. It is possible that Mark had several purposes, both evangelistic and pastoral. His overall aim is not hard to define: he wanted to persuade his readers to believe in "the gospel about Jesus Christ, the Son of God" (1:1), and to follow him.

He actually gives his book the title, "The beginning of the gospel about Jesus Christ" (1:1). Opinions differ about the significance of the word "beginning" here. Does it refer just to his introduction (1:1–15), or to the whole book? Since this is the opening sentence, it seems more likely that Mark is describing his whole book as "the beginning of the gospel." So he is assuming that his readers are already aware of the preaching of "the gospel," and of the community of believers who have committed themselves to it. He wants to tell them how it all started.

There are other indications that he knows he is not telling the whole story of "the gospel," and assumes knowledge of the later story among his readers:

- The promise of John the Baptist in 1:8, that Jesus will baptize with the Holy Spirit, is not fulfilled within the Gospel.

- Similarly, Jesus' promise to make his disciples into "fishers of men" (1:17) is not fulfilled within the Gospel.
- Neither is his promise in 14:28 to meet them in Galilee after the resurrection (unless this indicates that Mark's original did include the resurrection).
- He emphasizes the vital centrality of preaching and teaching in Jesus' ministry ("That is why I have come," 1:38), but records little more than summaries of its content. This suggests that both he and his readers knew that records of Jesus' teaching were available elsewhere.
- Mark's presentation of the disciples emphasizes their weakness, lack of understanding, fear, and unfaithfulness to such an extent that part of his message seems to be: just think what Jesus was able to do with this unpromising material later, after the Spirit was given! These disciples— particularly Peter—became the great leaders of the church. Mark himself had served alongside them, and knew from his own experience that "all things are possible with God" (10:27). Failure is not the last word.
- This sense of the continuing story is clearly discernible right at the end, with the final note of fear and disobedience in 16:8. Could "the gospel" end like this? Both Mark and his readers know that it did not. Far from it!

Mark's strategy, then, is to show "the beginning," the foundations, so that readers may understand why the message of Jesus Christ is "good news," and what in essence it means to follow him. We turn finally to a brief summary of his message.

Mark's Message

There are many facets to the message of such a brilliant book. However, we may summarize its main thrusts as follows:

1. The Kingdom of God

Mark summarizes Jesus' preaching as a message about the Kingdom of God: "After John was put in prison, Jesus went into Galilee, proclaiming the good news of God. 'The time has come,' he said. 'The kingdom of God is near. Repent and believe the good news!'" (Mark 1:14f.). Here "good news" is of course the word "gospel." Mark thus connects the "gospel" with a message about the nearness of the Kingdom of God, announced by Jesus.

We will consider the meaning of "the Kingdom of God" in the chapter on Matthew, because Matthew makes it more prominent a feature of Jesus' teaching than Mark. Whereas Matthew refers to "the Kingdom of heaven" some fifty times, Mark mentions it only fifteen times.

"The Kingdom of God" was a glowing future expectation for Jews (compare Mark 15:43). Whenever the Kingdom should come, it would mean the overthrow of God's enemies and the vindication of Israel as God's people. Against this background, we can summarize the message in Mark as follows:

- The Kingdom is near, about to arrive (1:15)!
- It is near because Jesus has come (11:10; compare 2:18–22).
- The process that will trigger its full appearance has already started (4:26,30).
- Contrary to current expectation, it is difficult to enter the Kingdom (10:24). It is certainly not automatic. Drastic action may be necessary (9:47). In fact, entry is open only to those who give up everything and follow Jesus (10:15, 21).

2. The death of Jesus

As we noted above, Mark's emphasis on the death of Jesus is one of the most striking features of his ground-breaking Gospel. What does he teach about it?

The Gospel begins with conflict. The conflict between Jesus and the religious establishment is signalled as early as Mark 1:22: "The people were amazed at his teaching, because he taught them as one who had authority, not as the teachers of the law." It quickly becomes clear that this note of authority will be regarded as blasphemous by the Pharisees (2:6). And when Jesus claims independent authority to associate with "sinners" (2:15-17), and to rewrite the rules governing fasting (2:18-22), Sabbath observance (2:23-28), and healing (3:1-5), the result is immediate and ominous: "Then the Pharisees went out and began to plot with the Herodians how they might kill Jesus" (3:6). By mentioning the collaboration of Pharisees and Herodians in the plot (normally at daggers drawn with each other), Mark underlines the strength of the opposition to Jesus.

The conflict is further underlined by the incident in 3:20-30, where "the teachers of the law" accuse Jesus of being demon-possessed, and he in turn accuses them of blasphemy against the Holy Spirit. In effect, they were accusing him of being a false prophet, the penalty for which was death (Deuteronomy 13:1-5), while he was accusing them of highhanded rebellion against the Lord like that of the sons of Eli, for which no atonement was possible (1 Samuel 2:25; 3:13f.). We wonder how long a final showdown can be delayed.

But in fact no attempt is made to kill Jesus, so long as he is in Galilee. Mark lets us know that the opposition to Jesus comes from Jerusalem (3:22), and reminds us of this again in chapter 7, when "the Pharisees and some of the teachers of the law who had come from Jerusalem" (7:1) accuse Jesus of teaching impurity, and he replies that they teach disobedience (7:5-9).

With this conflict lurking in the background, we are not surprised at the reaction of the disciples when Jesus decides to travel to Jerusalem: they "were astonished, while those who followed were afraid" (10:32).

By this time, however, two further developments have taken place. Firstly, the opposition to Jesus has spread. His family think he is mad (3:21). The Gerasenes want Jesus to go away (5:17). His home town takes offence at him (6:3). Even the disciples are in danger of being infected by "the yeast of the Pharisees" (8:15), and Peter tries to do Satan's work against Jesus (8:33). The trouble is that this is an "adulterous and sinful generation" (8:38), and all who belong to it—even Jesus' disciples—will ultimately oppose him.

The second development takes place suddenly and unexpectedly when Peter, speaking for all the disciples, calls Jesus "the Christ" (8:29). Jesus immediately announces his forthcoming death: "He then began to teach them that the Son of Man must suffer many things and be rejected by the elders, chief priests and teachers of the law, and that he must be killed and after three days rise again" (8:31). So what the Pharisees and Herodians are plotting for reasons of their own must happen, because it is *written* that the Son of Man must suffer much and be rejected" (9:12).

The action of the drama thus converges on Jerusalem with a tremendous sense of the inevitable. For altogether human and political reasons, the authorities want to kill Jesus, while he willingly moves into their trap for altogether heavenly and scriptural reasons. He repeats his prediction of his coming suffering, death, and resurrection on three further occasions before actually arriving in Jerusalem (9:31; 10:32–34; 10:45).

The last of these is particularly significant: "Whoever wants to become great among you must be your servant, and whoever wants to be first must be slave of all. For even the Son of Man did not come to be served, but to serve, and to give his life as a ransom for many" (10:43–45). Only here does Mark give us insight into the Scriptures in which it was *written* that the Christ must die. In this saying, Jesus draws on the language of Isaiah 53, and clearly identifies himself as the "servant of the Lord" who bears the sins of God's people as he is "despised and rejected" and brought to a violent death (53:3ff.).

Sure enough, the conflict with the authorities reaches a new intensity when Jesus starts to minister in Jerusalem (chapters 11–12). But the story takes a new, dramatic twist in 14:18–21, when Jesus suddenly announces that his death will not be caused just by the opposition of the religious authorities: one of the Twelve is going to betray him. The identity of the betrayer is not revealed, and all the disciples protest total loyalty. But in the end there is not much difference between Judas, who deserts him and joins the opposition, and the rest, who desert him and flee. And so, in the long run, there is not much difference between the disciples who acquiesce in his death, and his outright opponents who engineer it.

The point is that all, whether disciples or enemies, are equally in need of someone to die for them, someone to "give his life as a ransom" for their forgiveness. For Mark it is supremely his *death* which validates the claim that Jesus is "the Christ, the Son of God" (1:1). As soon as he dies, the centurion standing by the cross realizes the truth: "Surely this man was the Son of God!" (15:39).

3. *The cost of discipleship*

We have already considered Mark's interest in the difficulties and challenges of discipleship, and his sympathy for the weaknesses of the first apostles. But this sympathy does not lead him to lessen the demand laid on the disciples of Jesus. This may have been a temptation for him, in those earlier days when he fled from Pamphylia back to Jerusalem. Does Christian faith really demand such sacrifice?

But by the time he wrote his Gospel, Mark had faced and overcome his fear; and, perhaps as a result of this battle, he presents more sharply than the other evangelists the sheer cost demanded of the followers of Jesus:

"Then he called the crowd to him along with his disciples and said: 'If anyone would come after me, he must deny himself and take up his cross and follow me. For whoever wants to save his life will lose it, but whoever loses his life for me and for the gospel will save it'" (8:34f.).

Jesus issues this call immediately after announcing his own death for the first time. His disciples must go the same way, bearing their own cross, ready to lose their lives for him and for the gospel. The title of the autobiography of Frank Chikane, the General Secretary of the South African Council of Churches, will be the motto over their lives also: *No Life of My Own*!

What is meant by this self-denial is explained more clearly in Mark 10:17ff. The rich young man is challenged to "Go, sell everything you have and give to the poor, and you will have treasure in heaven. Then come, follow me" (10:21). But he is unwilling. Peter protests, "We have left everything to follow you!" (10:28), and then hears Jesus' promise that "no one who has left home or brothers or sisters or mother or father or children or fields for me and the gospel will fail to receive a hundred times as much in this present age (homes, brothers, sisters, mothers, children and fields—and with them, persecutions) and in the age to come, eternal life" (10:29f.).

The disciples lived in a culture in which home and family roots were very important. Indeed, Jews believed that their family land had been given to them by God, and so ultimately must not be given away or sold. Yet Jesus invites them to turn their backs on it all, for his sake. True, he promises that they will receive as much in return. But what they receive will not be the same as what they give up. They give up their human families; they receive the family of God (3:34f.). And they will also receive "persecutions," for they will be challenging an "adulterous and sinful generation" which still puts total store by what they renounce.

Not every Christian is called to leave home and family for Jesus' sake. But Mark was. He had to leave the security and wealth of his family home in Jerusalem and travel, first with Barnabas to

Cyprus, and thereafter we know not where, except that it included Asia Minor, and that he ended up in Rome with Peter and with Paul. He became "a fisher of men" with them, reaching out, like his Lord, to the needy and the lost, forgetful of himself, giving up everything that he might gain far more. And he draws people to Christ still, through his superb Gospel which speaks as vividly today as it did to Matthew and Luke when they were seeking inspiration for their own work.

CHAPTER 2

Matthew and His Message

Jesus went throughout Galilee, teaching in their synagogues, preaching the good news of the kingdom, and
healing every disease and sickness among the people.

(Matthew 4:23)

If Mark's is the Gospel of Christ the *suffering Servant,* and Luke's
the Gospel of Christ the *universal Savior,* Matthew's is the Gospel of Christ the *ruling King.* "The Kingdom of heaven" is the great
theme of Matthew's Gospel, but for Matthew its importance rests
on the identity of Jesus. Jesus is the King, who by his birth, by his
baptism, by his calling and teaching of the disciples, by his works
of power and mercy, and supremely by his death and resurrection,
has made the Kingdom of heaven both a present experience to
be enjoyed, and a future hope to be expected. (Matthew follows
Jewish custom in referring to "Kingdom of heaven," rather than
"Kingdom of God.")

For centuries Christians believed that Matthew's Gospel was
the first to be written, and therefore the most important of the
four. But over the last 150 years this view has largely been abandoned, and most scholars—though not all—now regard Mark's as
the first Gospel. The argument which has produced this change
of perspective can be stated easily. Of Mark's 662 verses, about
600 also appear in Matthew. It makes little sense to imagine Mark

creating a collection of 600 verses from Matthew, adding just a few further items, and then publishing it as a separate Gospel. It makes more sense to imagine Matthew using Mark as the basis for a much grander production. Basically following Mark's pattern, Matthew supplements it with further material which makes his Gospel almost twice the length of Mark (1,069 verses in total).

Because Matthew had this close relationship with Mark, we can identify some of the themes closest to his heart by paying special attention to the material he chose to add.

Who Was Matthew?

Like Mark, he keeps silent about his own identity. He was clearly a gifted teacher, who longed to communicate the teaching of Jesus and to encourage obedience to it. But for Matthew, this meant focusing all the attention on Jesus, and away from himself. He records Jesus' own words on this: "Nor are you to be called 'teacher,' for you have one Teacher, the Christ. The greatest among you will be your servant. For whoever exalts himself will be humbled, and whoever humbles himself will be exalted" (23:10–12). This was the pattern Matthew himself adopted, for there is no indication of authorship within the Gospel itself.

From the start, however, the title "According to Matthew" was attached to this Gospel by others. And, precisely because Matthew is such an obscure figure among the apostles, it is hard to see why his name was used, unless there was some solid reason for the tradition.

The first written testimony comes from Papias, the Bishop of Hierapolis whose "Explanation of the Lord's Words" was published around AD 130. He has long puzzled scholars with his comment, "Matthew carefully arranged [or 'collected'] the Lord's words in Hebrew dialect [or 'style'], and everyone interpreted them as best they could." In fact it seems unlikely that Matthew's

Gospel was originally written in Hebrew; it bears none of the typical marks which might suggest this. But, however puzzling Papias' testimony, he firmly identifies Matthew as the author of this Gospel.

Some scholars have rejected this ancient testimony, however, chiefly on the ground that Matthew, who was an apostle, would hardly have depended so extensively on the Gospel of Mark, who was not an apostle. But this objection

a. ignores the extent of Mark's literary achievement in creating the Gospel *form,*
b. does not allow for the real possibility that Matthew wanted to *endorse* Mark's work, which was based on the preaching of Peter, and
c. underestimates the extent to which Matthew's Gospel is very different from Mark's. It is by no means just an expansion or supplement of it, but tells the story in a distinctively "Matthean" way.

What do we know about Matthew? Can we trace any ways in which he was prepared by God to be the author of this Gospel? We have little certain knowledge about him, but we can gather more than appears at first sight when we read his Gospel in the light of what we know.

1. Matthew was a Jew

"Matthew" is a Hebrew name. Several of his fellow apostles had both a Hebrew name and a Greek name, expressing their double cultural roots. But Matthew's other name was also Hebrew. He is called "Levi" by Mark and Luke in their descriptions of his call by Jesus (Mark 2:14; Luke 5:27–29). His deep interest in the Old Testament is evident from his Gospel, as we shall see. One of his purposes in writing was undoubtedly to persuade fellow Jews to believe that Jesus is "the Christ, the Son of the living God" (16:16).

But, in early life, Matthew was a most unusual Jew. For—

2. *Matthew was a tax collector*

This is revealed in the one story in which he figures in his Gospel. "As Jesus went on from there, he saw a man named Matthew sitting at the tax collector's booth. 'Follow me,' he told him, and Matthew got up and followed him" (Matthew 9:9). From Mark and Luke we gather that it was Matthew who then threw the party at which Jesus and his disciples met "many tax collectors and 'sinners'" (9:10)—Matthew's former associates. He calls himself "Matthew the tax collector" in the list of apostles in Matthew 10:3.

What did it mean, to be a tax collector at that time? The Roman Empire had elaborate tax-collecting systems, which varied from place to place. At this time varying systems operated in Palestine; Judea, to the south, was directly governed from Rome, and this meant that the Roman governor and his civil servants were responsible for collecting all the main taxes. The chief of these were a poll tax levied on all adults, and a land tax. However, the rights to collect some minor taxes—chiefly customs dues at ports and on main roads—were sold off to the highest bidders.

Zacchaeus had bought the right to collect these taxes in Jericho (Luke 19:1–10). He is called "a chief tax collector" who "was wealthy" (19:2). We may imagine that he ran a sizeable organization, to cover the whole of the Jericho area, through which much trade passed.

Galilee, in the north, was ruled by Herod Antipas, under the overall authority of Rome. Here, Herod was responsible for collecting taxes, and for delivering a fixed lump sum annually to Rome. We do not know whether he charged the same kinds of tax as the Romans in Judea, but it is clear that he used a large workforce to collect it. "Many" tax collectors gathered in Matthew's house to meet Jesus, and we may imagine that only those in the immediate vicinity of Capernaum would have come.

We do not know whether Herod employed all his tax collectors directly as civil servants, or whether, like the Romans, he auctioned the right to collect taxes. Matthew's passing reference to Herod's "attendants" in 14:2 (only in Matthew) might suggest that he had been directly employed by the King: did he hear what Herod was saying about Jesus from one of his former colleagues?

But whether employed or freelance, tax collectors were highly unpopular and were regarded as traitors to the Jewish cause. Many of them used their position to raise extra money for themselves (indeed, this was one of the main purposes of buying the right to collect). But even if they did not, they were seen as collaborators with the Roman occupying power, or with Herod, who only ruled by Roman permission and was not a Jew himself.

Jews could only take on such a job if they loved money more than their national heritage as Jews. The Rabbis taught that it was perfectly in order to deceive a tax collector. They listed "tax-collecting" alongside prostitution among the occupations which no law-abiding Jew could undertake, since it meant dealing with Gentiles and working on the Sabbath, quite apart from greed and injustice.

Tax collectors thus formed a class apart, ostracized, outlawed from Jewish society. Their presence would have been unacceptable in the synagogues. So most tax collectors, for all these various reasons, had little interest in the Law, and in the worship of the God of Israel. They had set their hearts on earthly, not spiritual, riches.

From all of this we can form quite a clear picture of Matthew before he met Jesus. But the tax collector's usual negligence of Jewish tradition hardly squares with Matthew's Gospel, which abounds in Old Testament quotations and respect for the Law. How had Matthew developed this?

3. *Matthew experienced a revolutionary conversion*

His encounter with Jesus transformed his life. In some cases his fellow apostles continued to practice their professions after becoming disciples of Jesus. Peter maintained his home in Capernaum, and probably kept his fishing business going (compare John 21:3). But Matthew gave up tax collecting completely.

We gather this from two pieces of evidence. Firstly, with him in the group of the twelve apostles was "Simon the Zealot" (Matthew 10:4)—a former member of the revolutionary movement which opposed submission to Rome with violence. Before they both met Jesus, Simon would have regarded Matthew with deep hatred as a faithless collaborator. Matthew pointedly mentions both his own profession and Simon's in his list of the apostles in 10:2–4, to underline their reconciliation with each other. They could not have joined each other in this way if they had not both abandoned their former lives to follow Jesus.

Secondly, Matthew uniquely includes Jesus' direct teaching on the payment of tax (17:24–27). Only he records this incident in which Jesus pays his Temple tax (a levy on all adult Jews to maintain the Temple and its services) by sending Peter out to find a coin in the mouth of a fish. The interpretation of this passage is disputed, but the most likely is that Jesus is declaring the fundamental freedom, both of himself and of his followers, from all tax obligations. They are the children of God, who is the King of all the earth. So they are "free" from such bondage. Yet God will provide the means to pay such taxes, just in order to avoid giving unnecessary offence to society around.

We may guess that Matthew included this story because it meant much to him. He had been set free from bondage to that whole system—in fact, set free from serving Mammon, the God of money (6:24).

We will consider below how his conversion may have affected Matthew and the Gospel he wrote. But it is worth asking further about that conversion itself: Why was he so willing to stand up and leave his business that day, when he heard just two words from Jesus: "Follow me"?

The answer may lie in another figure who plays a prominent role in his Gospel:

4. Matthew had probably been deeply affected by John the Baptist

This is speculative, but the evidence points in this direction.

Only Matthew includes the parable of the Two Sons in 21:28–32. Here the first son, who refuses to work in his father's vineyard but then repents and goes, is interpreted as "the tax collectors and the prostitutes" who responded to the preaching of John the Baptist. They are now "entering the kingdom of God ahead of" the religious leaders, who did not "repent and believe" John. "The vineyard" is an Old Testament picture for Israel, God's people (e.g. Isaiah 5:1–7).

Does this reflect Matthew's own experience? Was he among the tax collectors who, according to Luke, came to be baptized by John? When they asked John how they should show their repentance, he told them, "Don't collect any more than you are required to" (Luke 3:13).

Repentance for Matthew could have been much fuller than just cutting out over-charging. Perhaps this was the point at which he became much more serious about the Law, convicted by John of his disregard of it, ready to study and obey it in a new way—in fact, ready to enter the vineyard, repenting of his disobedience. He would also have heard John's testimony to Jesus, "After me will come one who is more powerful than I, whose sandals I am not fit to carry . . ." (Matthew 3:11), and would have been watching for him. Matthew heard Jesus preach as he went "throughout Galilee" (4:23) repeating the message of John, "Repent, for the kingdom of heaven is near" (4:17; compare 3:2). Gradually he was prepared for a further step, from John the Baptist to Jesus.

So it seems likely that Matthew's conversion went through two stages, first to the Law, prompted by John the Baptist, and then to the Christ, prompted by that two-word summons. Suddenly Matthew knew that he must give up all and follow Jesus. Within a few weeks he found himself sent out on a mission with his fellow disciples, and told to make no provision for the journey, no protection against danger, and no prior arrangements for hospitality (Matthew 10:9-11). Matthew emphasizes much more than Mark and Luke the self-sacrifice and helplessness which Jesus required of the disciples on that mission. This must have been especially difficult for Matthew, and must have underlined for him the vast change that had taken place in his life. From wealth to deliberate poverty, from self-determination to discipleship, from safety to a life of dangerous faith, above all from self to Christ—this was Matthew's conversion.

May we discern other ways in which this conversion affected both Matthew and his Gospel?

The New Matthew

Three important features of Matthew's Gospel may be traced back to this conversion experience.

1. He learned about mercy and forgiveness

These are important themes in his Gospel. Matthew uses the term "debts" rather than "sins" in the version of the Lord's Prayer he records: "Forgive us our debts, as we also have forgiven our debtors" (Matthew 6:12; compare Luke 11:4). As a tax collector, he had never forgiven debts—how could he? But he had come to realize the vast, unpaid debt which he owed to God, the debt of love and obedience.

Only Matthew records the parable of the Unforgiving Servant (Matthew 18:23–35). In his former life he must have frequently acted out the role of the servant: "He grabbed him and began to choke him. 'Pay back what you owe me!' he demanded" (18:28). Matthew may never have behaved so violently, but he must have been used to putting pressure on people to pay, even when they could barely do so. Now, however, he has learned the lesson of that parable. Of far greater importance is the debt owed to God, and we owe him far, far more than we can ever pay. If we simply accept forgiveness from him as a gift, can we then refuse to forgive others?

Similarly, only Matthew records the parable of the Workers in the Vineyard (20:1–16). Doubtless he had heard such complaints of unfairness many times, and perhaps had treated people unjustly himself. But now the paradox impresses him deeply: unjustly, unfairly, he has received the goodness of God, who does not unjustly demand, but unjustly gives far more than we deserve (20:15).

There must have been plenty of forgiveness given and received among the apostles as they settled down together in their new life as disciples of Jesus. Matthew came from Capernaum, like Peter and Andrew, and James and John. He was "their" tax collector—or at any rate known to them as such. There may have been old arguments to settle, sins to confess, injustices to right. Certainly Matthew and Simon the Zealot had much to repent of mutually.

One verse seems to have meant much to Matthew in connection with all this. Twice he records Jesus' quotation of Hosea 6:6, "I desire mercy, not sacrifice." None of the other evangelists mention Jesus' use of this verse. On the first occasion, Matthew describes how Jesus quoted this verse in his own home, at the dinner-party which he threw for his former colleagues, just after he had become a disciple. Some local Pharisees made it clear that they disapproved of the event by asking Jesus' other disciples, "Why does your teacher eat with tax collectors and 'sinners'?" (9:11). Matthew discovered that the Pharisees disliked Jesus as much as they had disliked him.

Jesus' reply clearly stuck in his memory: "It is not the healthy who need a doctor, but the sick. But go and learn what this means: 'I desire mercy, not sacrifice.' For I have not come to call the righteous, but sinners" (9:12f.). From Jesus he had received that mercy—not just in that Jesus had been willing to associate with him, but much more because, through Jesus, he knew that his enormous, unpayable debt had been cancelled. The years he had spent in disobedience and greed had been forgiven.

Matthew records a further use of Hosea 6:6 by Jesus when he was later criticized by the Pharisees for allowing his disciples to rub corn in their hands on the Sabbath (12:1f.). After giving some scriptural examples of similar Sabbath-breaking (12:3–6), Jesus concludes, "If you had known what these words mean, 'I desire mercy, not sacrifice,' you would not have condemned the innocent. For the Son of Man is Lord of the Sabbath" (12:7f.). The mercy that Matthew had so often withheld as a tax collector now moved center-stage in his life. But further he learned that Jesus is the one who decides what mercy is, and how it shall be shown—in fact, how Scriptures like Hosea 6:6 are to be interpreted. Jesus—the "Son of Man"—is the Lord who decides such things. Jesus as the sovereign interpreter of Scripture is a central theme in Matthew's teaching, as we shall see.

2. He developed a new view of the King

We do not know whether Matthew the tax collector had ever been an enthusiastic "Herodian"—the name given to the monarchist party which championed the dynasty of the Herods (compare Matthew 22:16; Mark 3:6). But if he had been, his conversion marked a dramatic change here also. Matthew the evangelist placed no confidence whatever in political authority. In fact, quite the reverse. He records Jesus' distress over Israel more emphatically than the other evangelists: "When he saw the crowds, he had compassion on them, because they were harassed and helpless, like sheep without a shepherd" (9:36). Herod's rule left his people effectively shepherdless, harassed, and lost.

But God has acted to save his people. Matthew presents Jesus, in contrast to Herod, as the true King of Israel. Right at the start, he gives Herod his full title, "King Herod," as he introduces "the one who has been born king of the Jews" (2:1–2). Herod realizes the threat to his position, and does his best to murder this rival King (2:16–18). But he fails—and fails also to postpone his own immediate death, which Matthew records perhaps with a touch of wry humor (2:19).

Scholars have often commented on the prominence of the theme of kingship in Matthew. Its importance is signaled in Matthew's very first verse, which forms his own title to the Gospel: "A record of [or literally 'The book of'] the genealogy of Jesus Christ the son of David, the son of Abraham" (1:1).

David and Abraham are singled out as Jesus' chief ancestors. The genealogy which follows in Matthew 1:2–17 is then carefully constructed to lay emphasis on Jesus as the promised King: "Thus there were fourteen generations in all from Abraham to David, fourteen from David to the exile to Babylon, and fourteen from the exile to the Christ" (1:17). Jesus is "the Son of David" who revives the line of kings broken 600 years previously when the Babylonians sacked Jerusalem. He fulfills all the promises given by the prophets that a great "David" would come to rule not just Israel but the whole world. Following this, "Son of David" had become the standard name used by the Rabbis to refer to the Messiah (compare Matthew 22:42).

This is also one of Matthew's favorite titles for Jesus. He records its use on ten occasions (whereas Mark and Luke only muster seven between them). It has a special connection with acts of mercy towards the sick and the poor, for this was one of the chief roles of the king in the Old Testament: he was expected to be the defender of the weak and the helpless.

So what "King" Herod failed to do, Jesus fulfills perfectly. Herod never in fact claimed to be "son of David." He could not, for he was an Idumean, not a Jew, owing his throne entirely to the Romans, and for this reason many Jews disputed his title and rejected his rule. Matthew had moved from the service of a false and useless pretender to serve the true King of Israel.

This "true King of Israel" ruled over far more than just Herod's tiny kingdom. It was part of Old Testament expectation that the coming "David" would be a universal King. Here Matthew's tax-collecting background may even have helped him a little, for he would have rubbed shoulders with many non-Jews, and it may therefore have been easier for him than for others to accept that Gentiles would be brought in to enjoy the rule of this King.

We will look at Matthew's "Kingship" theme in more detail below, when we turn to the main features of his message.

3. He discovered a new gift for teaching

As we saw above, it is highly unlikely that Matthew the tax collector would have had any opportunity even to study the Law to any depth, let alone teach it. And yet his Gospel is clearly the product of someone both in love with the Law, and gifted as a teacher. We must conclude, then, that Matthew discovered a gift of which he had not been aware when his life was given to the pursuit of money.

What is the evidence for Matthew's teaching ability? We may point to four features of his Gospel:

a. His structured narrative

We have noted already Matthew's emphasis on Jesus' teaching, which is presented in five great sermons. These tend to treat distinct themes. Matthew or others may have compiled them by drawing together sayings on related themes, or they may have been based on talks actually given by Jesus. As a highly literate tax collector, Matthew could have taken notes as he listened to Jesus. Either way, we can easily imagine the usefulness of these compilations as a means of teaching young converts the basics of Christian life and faith.

b. His use of the Old Testament

Matthew betrays a teacher's love of pointing to the connection between prophecies and their fulfillment in Jesus. On no fewer than eleven occasions he links an event to a prophecy with a statement such as, "This took place to fulfill what was spoken through the prophet . . ." (21:4). If the suggestion above is correct—that he first found the Law through John the Baptist, and then the Gospel through Jesus—then it would help us to understand his fresh and unusual perspective on the Law. He interprets it in a unique way, looking at it through the spectacles of Christian faith and discipleship.

Again, we will look in more detail at this below.

c. His concern about the Pharisees

This is the counterpart of the last point. More than any other Gospel-writer, Matthew is critical of the Pharisees and their teaching. "Hostile" is the word used by many scholars in reaction to passages like Matthew 23:27f.: "Woe to you, teachers of the law and Pharisees, you hypocrites! You are like whitewashed tombs, which look beautiful on the outside but on the inside are full of dead men's bones and everything unclean. In the same way, on the outside you appear to people as righteous but on the inside you are full of hypocrisy and wickedness."

The other Gospel-writers hesitated to include the series of "Woes" directed at the Pharisees from which this comes (23:1–36). But Matthew does not hesitate. Yet he does not include these sayings out of hostility so much as out of concern at the dreadful effect of the Pharisees' teaching:

- "The teachers of the law and the Pharisees sit in Moses' seat. So you must obey them and do everything they tell you. But do not do what they do, for they do not practice what they preach. They tie up heavy loads and put them on men's shoulders, but they themselves are not willing to lift a finger to move them" (23:2–4).
- "Woe to you, teachers of the law and Pharisees, you hypocrites! You shut the kingdom of heaven in men's faces. You yourselves do not enter, nor will you let those enter who are trying to!" (23:13).

The Pharisees were legitimate teachers, but their message was lifeless and deathly to all who followed it. Matthew longed to replace their teaching with his.

d. His narrative style

Though Matthew's Gospel is so much longer than Mark's, he usually tells the same stories much more briefly. Whereas Mark includes many personal details, Matthew prunes the narrative to its bare essentials, but then frequently expands the "teaching" drawn from the story.

For instance, Mark tells the story of the demon-possessed boy in 256 words, up to the point where the disciples ask Jesus, "Why couldn't we drive it out?" (Mark 9:14–28). Jesus' answer to this question in Mark is simply, "This kind can come out only by prayer" (9:29). Matthew, in contrast, uses only 102 words to tell the story to the same point (17:14–20), but then records Jesus' reply much more fully: "Because you have so little faith. I tell you the truth, if you have faith as small as a mustard seed, you can say to this mountain, 'Move from here to there' and it will move. Nothing will be impossible for you" (17:20).

In all these ways Matthew's passion for teaching and discipling is expressed. He was working to obey the command of Jesus which he himself records, to "make disciples of all nations" (28:19). Perhaps he thought of himself as like the "teacher of the law who has been instructed about the kingdom of heaven" in 13:52 (again, this little parable is only in Matthew). He is "like the owner of a house who brings out of his storeroom new treasures as well as old." Matthew drew on the riches of the Old Testament to expound the gripping new wealth of Jesus, who is the pearl "of great value" for whom Matthew had sold up everything (13:45f.).

Matthew's Message

What, then, was the message which burned in Matthew's heart as he wrote his Gospel?—the message which his experience of Jesus had prepared him to proclaim? We may summarize it under five headings:

1. Jesus is the fulfillment of the Old Testament

This feature of Matthew's presentation of Jesus underlies all the others. Throughout his Gospel, what God is doing in and through

Jesus is explained and interpreted with reference to the Scriptures. Matthew assumes that his readers will be familiar with the Old Testament, and able to draw conclusions from the quotations with which he peppers the story.

For instance, Matthew follows Mark in reporting Jesus' evening healings (Mark 1:32–34), but then adds a quotation:

> When evening came, many who were demon-possessed were brought to him, and he drove out the spirits with a word and healed all the sick. This was to fulfill what was spoken through the prophet Isaiah: "He took up our infirmities and carried our diseases." (Matthew 8:16f.)

Matthew's readers are expected to know where this quotation is found in Isaiah. It is part of the description of the "Servant of the Lord" in Isaiah 53, who bears not only the sicknesses of God's people but also their sins, and dies on their behalf. By this brief quotation Matthew tells his readers that Jesus is this figure predicted by Isaiah—an important and dramatic claim. In 12:15–21, Matthew quotes at length from one of the "Servant Songs" in Isaiah (Isaiah 42:1–4), again applying it to Jesus.

Matthew 5:17–20 is a most important passage in this connection. "Do not think that I have come to abolish the Law or the Prophets; I have not come to abolish them but to fulfill them," Jesus says (5:17). By his behavior and teaching many thought that Jesus was opposing his authority to that of the Old Testament. Matthew wants to put the record straight. Jesus wanted to remove "not the smallest letter, not the least stroke of a pen" from the Law "until everything is accomplished" (5:18).

But this does not mean that current ways of interpreting the Law are accepted. Far from it. We have already seen Matthew's highly critical attitude towards the Pharisees, the contemporary guardians of Jewish orthodoxy. In the rest of chapter 5, Matthew records Jesus' reinterpretation of the Law in six areas. In some cases the reinterpretation is so far-reaching that it is almost as though the Law itself, and not just the Pharisees' application of it, is being set aside. Such is the note of authority with which Jesus teaches. The authority of Jesus is equal with the Law, but does not replace it. However, because of his authority as King and Son of God, the Law is reshaped and re-angled, so that instead of emphasizing the *difference* between Israel and the Gentile nations, the Law is now seen to *encourage* love for enemies (5:38–48) and a breaking down of the barrier between Jews and Gentiles (see here especially 15:1–28).

For whom did Matthew design this presentation? Most scholars believe that he had Christians in mind, perhaps especially Jewish Christians who needed to be convinced that their Christian faith was not in conflict with their Jewish heritage. But it seems likely that Matthew also wanted to convince unbelieving Jews, and that it was part of his strategy to show that Jesus perfectly fulfills Old Testament expectation. That Matthew had Jews in mind is suggested by 27:62–66 and 28:11–15, where Matthew takes pains to explain the origin, and falsity, of the current Jewish explanation of the resurrection. We discover from the second-century Christian apologist Justin Martyr, who wrote around AD 135, that Jews were still saying that the disciples had stolen the body of Jesus from the tomb. If Matthew wanted to reply to this false charge, then it seems likely that other features of his Gospel, and in particular his treatment of the Old Testament, would also be aimed at convincing skeptical Jews.

We shall discover more about Matthew's treatment of the Law as we trace his other central themes:

2. Jesus is the King!

"From that time on Jesus began to preach, 'Repent, for the kingdom of heaven is near'" (Matthew 4:17). It has long been recognized that "the kingdom of heaven" is a crucial theme in Matthew. It is important for all the evangelists, but above all for Matthew. He uses the expression fifty times, compared with Mark's fifteen, and Luke's thirty-eight.

When we put alongside this statistic the prominence of the royal title "Son of David," we clearly see how important for Matthew is the presentation of Jesus as the King.

A brief consideration of the Old Testament background is necessary here. God is frequently pictured as "King" in the Old Testament, and his "Kingdom" is a potent theme in Old Testament theology. The Greek and Hebrew words generally translated "kingdom" both have an interesting double meaning which is most important for understanding both the Old Testament and Jesus' proclamation. They mean both "realm" and "rule," both what the King does (he reigns) and where he does it (in his kingdom). In the Old Testament, this means that

a. God is pictured as reigning over the whole world (e.g. Psalm 47; 98:4–6; 99:1);
b. Israel is thought of as specially God's realm, the place where his kingship is most clearly expressed (e.g. 1 Samuel 8:7; 12:12; Psalm 48:1f.);
c. a day is expected when all the nations will submit to God's rule, that is, when his realm will be extended to cover the whole earth, just as he now reigns especially over Israel. This coming Kingdom will also mark the final deliverance of Israel herself (e.g. Psalm 47:7–9; Isaiah 52:7–10; Zechariah 9:9–12).

This expected Kingdom of God is marked by four characteristics in the Old Testament: *justice* (e.g. Jeremiah 23:5f.), *peace* (e.g. Ezekiel 34:23–31), *stability* (e.g. Isaiah 9:7), and *universality* (e.g. Zechariah 9:10).

In Jesus' day the expectation of this coming "Kingdom of God" was strong, but opinions varied about how it would come.

Some understood it politically, and looked forward to a day when Israel would be saved from all her enemies and be vindicated in the eyes of the world. Some even thought that they could hasten the coming of the Kingdom by taking up arms against the Romans. But others understood it spiritually, and looked for a time when God would finally save Israel from sin, and bring the Gentile nations to know him also.

So when Jesus announced "the kingdom of heaven is near" (4:17), people responded eagerly. But they needed to learn what Jesus' understanding of the Kingdom was: political or spiritual? Matthew likewise needed to unpack the nature of this Kingdom clearly for his readers. He says four things about it:

a. It focusses on the spiritual renewal of Israel

Matthew shows Jesus ministering almost exclusively to Israel. "I was sent only to the lost sheep of Israel," he says (15:24; compare 10:5f.). Similarly, Jesus sends out his disciples with the words, "Do not go among the Gentiles or enter any town of the Samaritans. Go rather to the lost sheep of Israel. As you go, preach this message: 'The kingdom of heaven is near'" (10:5–7).

But he then recognizes that, in fact, they will go "before governors and kings as witnesses to them and to the Gentiles" (10:18). The gospel which starts life addressed just to Israel is to spread. So Matthew gives prominence to the story of the centurion, who has faith greater than anyone in Israel (8:10), foreshadowing the "many" who will "come from the east and the west, and will take their places at the feast with Abraham, Isaac, and Jacob in the kingdom of heaven. But the subjects of the kingdom will be thrown outside . . ." (8:11f.). Israel ought to be there, but has not responded with the necessary faith. So Gentiles are to be brought in, to share the Kingdom banquet with Abraham. When the invited guests refuse to come, the servants are sent out to gather "all the people they could find, both good and bad, and the wedding hall was filled with guests" (22:10). This is exactly what Jesus then does, at the end of the Gospel (28:18–20).

b. It focusses around Jesus himself

Because Jesus is the King, the Kingdom—that is, the rule he exercises—arrives with him. Matthew links the Kingdom closely with Jesus' ministry of healing: "Jesus went through all the towns and villages, teaching in their synagogues, preaching the good news of the kingdom, and healing every disease and sickness" (9:35). His miracles point to the power of the Kingdom, present in him: "If I drive out demons by the Spirit of God, then the kingdom of God has come upon you" (12:28). It falls to John to describe Jesus' miracles as "signs," that is, special actions which incorporate a message and are thus part of his preaching and teaching. But they have this quality in Matthew, too. They mark Jesus out specifically as the one who fulfills the prophecy of Isaiah: "He took up our infirmities, and carried our diseases" (8:17). This therefore makes Jesus' miracles uniquely his, and not necessarily something to be expected wherever the Kingdom is proclaimed.

c. The followers of Jesus enter it already

When people step under the rule of this King, they enter the Kingdom. John the Baptist started the process: "From the days of John the Baptist until now, the kingdom of heaven has been forcefully advancing, and forceful men lay hold of it" (11:12). By "forceful" here, Jesus probably expresses the enthusiastic response of so many to his ministry. By following him, people are "laying hold of" the Kingdom of heaven—literally "snatching it up," like shoppers finding the bargain of a lifetime. Once inside, even the least in the Kingdom of heaven is greater than John the Baptist (11:11).

The rich young man is not so sure. He wants "eternal life" (this is an expression equivalent to "the Kingdom of God"), but he cannot cope with the condition: "Go, sell your possessions and give to the poor, and you will have treasure in heaven. Then come, follow me" (19:21). To follow Jesus is to do what he missed: "to enter the kingdom of heaven" (19:23).

A new lifestyle is demanded of these followers of Jesus, one which points to the reality of the Kingdom in them. This is why the Twelve, when sent out to preach the Kingdom, are told, "Freely you have received, freely give. Do not take along any gold or silver or copper in your belts; take no bag for the journey, or extra tunic, or sandals or a staff; for the worker is worth his keep" (10:8-10). God supplies everything they need for their sustenance and protection, and everything they have to give away. They are in themselves living sermons, evidence of the reality of the Kingdom they proclaim. Matthew takes great pains to spell out this new lifestyle for his readers, by recording Jesus' teaching at such length.

d. It is yet to "come"

Luke, in fact, emphasizes the presence of the Kingdom more than Matthew. Matthew's distinctive emphasis falls on the Kingdom that is yet to be. Jesus, as "the Son of Man," is to come again in mighty power and in judgment, and this will happen soon. "I tell you the truth, some who are standing here will not taste death before they see the Son of Man coming in his kingdom" (16:28).

This "coming of the Son of Man" forms the subject of chapters 24-25. The interpretation of these chapters is much disputed, especially that of chapter 24, but nearly all agree that two kinds of "coming" are being linked and treated together in these chapters:

- On the one hand there is a *coming in judgment,* which will mean the fulfillment of Jesus' prediction that the Temple will be destroyed: "Not one stone here will be left on another; every one will be thrown down" (24:2). This is probably the "coming of the Son of Man" which is to take place within a generation (24:34).
- On the other hand, there is a further *coming in glory* (25:31), which will herald the final judgment of the world and the salvation of God's people. "The King" (25:34)—that is, Jesus—will pass judgment on the nations gathered before him, ushering "the righteous" into eternal life, and "the cursed" into eternal punishment (25:46).

3. Jesus is the Son of God!

One of the leading writers on Matthew, Professor Jack Kingsbury, argues that "the Son of God" is, in Matthew's mind, the most important title given to Jesus. Whether it is more important than other titles is open to dispute, but its significance cannot be doubted. It is used effectively on fourteen occasions in Matthew.

It is almost always used about Jesus by others:

- By the devil or demons: 4:3, 6; 8:29
- By Jesus' enemies in accusation or mockery: 26:63; 27:40, 43
- By Matthew, the disciples, or others in confession of faith: 2:15; 14:33; 16:16; 27:54
- By God himself: 3:17; 17:5; 21:37

On just two occasions Jesus himself refers to "the Son": 24:36; 28:19.

As a title it has three connotations:

a. It connotes Israel

In the Old Testament the whole nation is thought of as "the son of God" (e.g. Exodus 4:22). Matthew quotes one such passage and applies it to Jesus. Hosea 11:1, quoted in 2:15, referred originally to the exodus: "Out of Egypt I called my son." Some scholars have suspected Matthew of wild proof-texting here, as though Matthew had little concern for the original meaning. But nothing could be further from the truth. Throughout these opening chapters of the Gospel, Matthew is at pains to show how Jesus steps into the shoes of Israel, and repeats Israel's experience. He comes out of Egypt, is rescued from a hostile king who tries to exterminate him, passes through water, is tested and tempted in the wilderness, and eventually arrives at a mountain where God's word is heard (5:1).

There are differences, of course. Whereas Israel failed the test in the wilderness (compare Deuteronomy 8:5), this Son of God passes with flying colors. And whereas Israel heard the word of God at Mount Sinai, this Son of God speaks it. But the parallels are clear. Jesus takes upon himself the role of Israel, so as to re-form the people of God around himself. One day, his apostles will sit on thrones beside him, judging the tribes of Israel (Matthew 19:28).

b. It connotes royalty

The title "Son of God" was also borne by the king in the Old Testament (compare 2 Samuel 7:14; Psalm 2:7). With this in the background, the application of this title to Jesus must link in with the other "royal" themes in Matthew—especially "Kingdom," and "Son of David."

c. It connotes deity

As in John's Gospel, the title "Son of God" points to a relationship of the deepest intimacy with God. On nine occasions Jesus refers to "my heavenly Father" or "my Father in heaven," and in one famous passage (only in Matthew) specifies what this relationship means:

> I praise you, Father, Lord of heaven and earth, because you have hidden these things from the wise and learned, and revealed them to little children. Yes, Father, for this was your good pleasure. All things have been committed to me by my Father. No one knows the Son except the Father, and no one knows the Father except the Son and those to whom the Son chooses to reveal him. (11:25–27)

Jesus enjoys a unique relationship of knowledge, giving, and mutual activity with God his Father. But while it is unique, it is also shared. For on no fewer than eleven occasions Jesus refers to "your heavenly Father" or "your Father in heaven" when addressing his disciples. Matthew rejoiced in the new intimacy with God which following Jesus had brought to him. No longer was God a judge to be feared, but a Father to be trusted.

4. Jesus is the teacher, the Christ!

Matthew connects these two titles in 23:10. Jesus as a teacher is uniquely important for him, as we have already seen. And, putting together the subjects covered by Jesus' five great sermons, Matthew has clearly sought to provide a rounded presentation of Christian faith and discipleship. For instance, he alone gives teaching on the thorny issue of church discipline (18:15–35). In fact, only Matthew records Jesus' use of the term "church" (16:18;

18:17). From Matthew and Mark we might gain the impression that Jesus never intended to found the church, but Matthew will not permit this. Undoubtedly, he had the needs of the church in his own day in mind as he selected and ordered his material.

5. Jesus is the Savior, the Son of Man!

Like the other evangelists, Matthew lays great emphasis on the suffering and death of Jesus. He did not just come to re-interpret the Old Testament and give new teaching from God—very far from it. Matthew includes the saying so important for Mark: "Whoever wants to be first must be your slave—just as the Son of Man did not come to be served, but to serve, and to give his life as a ransom for many" (20:27f.). He too interprets Jesus' death in advance by recording his words at the last supper: "This is my blood of the covenant, which is poured out for many for the forgiveness of sins" (26:28). Through his death, Jesus forges a whole new covenant between God and his people, taking away their sins just as the angel had promised to Joseph: "You are to give him the name Jesus, because he will save his people from their sins" (1:21).

This emphasis connects with the distinctive theme we noted above, that of mercy to the weak. Matthew's is a very tender Gospel:

- Only he records Jesus' great words, "Come to me, all you who are weary and burdened, and I will give you rest. Take my yoke upon you and learn from me, for I am gentle and humble in heart, and you will find rest for your souls. For my yoke is easy and my burden is light" (11:28–30).
- Normally he shortens stories drawn from Mark. But in the case of the story of the man with the withered hand, he expands it with another famous saying: "If any of you has a sheep and it falls into a pit on the Sabbath, will you not take

hold of it and lift it out? How much more valuable is a man than a sheep!" (12:11f.).

- Supremely, he brings the last block of teaching to a great climax with the parable of the Sheep and the Goats (again, only recorded by Matthew). The Son of Man, the King before whom the nations of the world are divided and by whom their destiny is decided, has made himself hungry and thirsty, alienated and naked, sick and rejected, and shares all these experiences with his "brothers." No suffering disciple is distant from him, but he knows and bears it all as well.

Matthew's Gospel is certainly that of the ruling King, as we described it at the start of this chapter. But this King is different from all others. He does not rule with distant authority and live in separate splendor. He sits on a throne and judges the nations (25:31f.), but only because "he took up our infirmities and carried our diseases" (8:17, quoting Isaiah 53:4). He rules as a servant, not with power but with compassion, not in self-protection but in total self-giving. This is the beating heart of Matthew's Gospel message—the message which drew him from greed and self-service into the life and service of this King.

CHAPTER 3

Luke and His Message

He told them, "This is what is written: The Christ will suffer and rise from the dead on the third day, and repentance and forgiveness of sins will be preached in his name to all nations, beginning at Jerusalem. You are witnesses of these things."

(Luke 24:46–48)

Luke's Gospel is in many ways the most distinctive of the three synoptic Gospels, and, since he is the author of the Acts of the Apostles as well, Luke's literary contribution to the New Testament is greater than that of any other writer (more than a quarter of the whole). The Gospel and Acts together constitute a single, two-volume work, the over-riding theme of which is the universality of the Kingdom of God. So Luke traces the story of the coming of the Kingdom from its beginnings with John the Baptist through to its proclamation in Rome, the heart of the empire. Looking on the new-born Jesus, Simeon praises God: "For my eyes have seen your salvation, which you have prepared in the sight of all people, a light for revelation to the Gentiles . . ." (Luke 2:30–32). Luke tells the story of the spreading of this light until, two volumes later, his work concludes with Paul's words, "I want you to know that God's salvation has been sent to the Gentiles, and they will listen!" (Acts 28:28).

Luke the Man

Luke was personally well-equipped to tell this story. We may summarize what we know about him as follows:

1. Luke was a Gentile

In fact, he was the only Gentile among the New Testament writers. "Luke" is a Latin name (a shortened form of the name "Lucius"). Several further factors indicate Luke's Gentile origins:

a. When Paul sends greetings to the Colossian Christians he mentions three of his companions by name as "the only Jews among my fellow workers for the kingdom of God." Then he sends greetings from three others, who are presumably not Jewish. Among them is "our dear friend Luke, the doctor" (Colossians 4:10–14).

b. Whenever he quotes from the Old Testament Luke uses the Greek version and does not translate direct from the Hebrew. He refers four times to "the Aramaic language" in ways that give the impression that he could not speak it (Acts 1:19; 21:40; 22:2; 26:14).

c. There is an early church tradition that he came from Antioch in Syria, one of the largest cities in the Roman Empire. We cannot be sure of the truth of this, but he certainly shows much interest in the birth and growth of the church in Antioch (Acts 11:19–30), and does not let us forget that it was the apostle Paul's "home" church (Acts 13:1–3; 14:26–28).

d. His two-volume work is unique in the New Testament in being dedicated to a patron, Theophilus (Luke 1:3; Acts 1:1). This was a common practice in the Graeco-Roman world, and was also adopted by some Jewish writers, such as the historian Josephus, who wished to attract a Gentile readership for his history of the Jewish people. But Josephus' dedication of his work to his patron Epaphroditus is ponderous and affected in comparison with Luke's simple and natural address to his patron.

Scholars used to speculate on the identity of Theophilus; and if, as some of them thought, he was a wealthy aristocratic Roman, then Luke himself must have moved in such circles—perhaps in the expatriate Roman community in Antioch. But the name "Theophilus" means "lover of God," and may be a pseudonym, perhaps addressing any who, like Cornelius (Acts 10:1–2), were devout and God-fearing Gentiles, genuine seekers of the truth. Luke knew how to address such people, and how to convince them of the "certainty" of the truth about Jesus (Luke 1:4).

2. Luke was highly educated

He would need to be, as a doctor. One older scholar speculates that Luke received his medical training in Tarsus, Paul's home town, which was a great center of learning. At that time medicine was a special branch of philosophy, and Luke's general culture and education are clear in his writings.

For instance, he has a rich vocabulary. Luke and Acts have about 800 words which do not occur elsewhere in the New Testament. His Greek is good: after that of the letter to the Hebrews, the most elegant in the New Testament. And it is also flexible: Luke shows considerable literary artistry, for instance, in the way in which he is able to write his preface in high, classical Greek (Luke 1:1–4), and then immediately switch to a very different style, one modeled on that of the Greek Old Testament, for the stories of Jesus' birth and childhood. In this way, he communicates a sense of time and place to his Gentile readers, as well as the facts and the truths.

Going beyond the style of Luke's Greek, scholars have devoted much attention to the literary skill with which he composes the story. He modestly calls his work "an orderly account" (Luke 1:3), and the "order" is apparent in the beautiful way in which the story develops. For instance, the importance of Jesus' death and resurrection is underlined in the Gospel by the repeated references to Jesus' journey to Jerusalem, starting in 9:51: "As the time approached for him to be taken up to heaven, Jesus resolutely set out for Jerusalem . . . ." After this point, even innocent references to Jesus' walking along the road (e.g. 9:57; 10:38; 11:53) take on powerful, dramatic force.

Luke was certainly a consummate literary artist.

3. Luke was a historian

According to 1:3, his "orderly account" is based on painstaking research: "I myself have carefully investigated everything from the beginning." So his literary artistry went hand-in-hand with a concern for accuracy and therefore reliability.

This accuracy was powerfully vindicated in the early years of the twentieth century through the research of Sir William Ramsay, who as a student had imbibed the view, at that time widely held by scholars, that Luke's Gospel was written in the second century AD by an author who freely invented much of his material. But Ramsay's ground-breaking studies of the area and cities covered by Paul's first and second missionary journeys (Acts 13–18) completely changed his mind. Luke had shown meticulous accuracy in matters of geography and civil administration—in fact, in every detail where he could be tested. In his book *The Bearing of Recent Discovery on the Trustworthiness of the New Testament,* published in 1915, Ramsay concluded, "You may press the words of Luke in a degree beyond any other historian's, and they stand the keenest scrutiny and the hardest treatment." He suggested that this demonstrable accuracy should affect our attitude to Luke's whole work: "There is a certain presumption that a writer who proves to be exact and correct in one point will show the same qualities in other matters. No writer is correct by mere chance, or accurate sporadically. He is accurate by virtue of a certain habit of mind."

Luke clearly had a mind of that type. Many other scholars today are ready to accept this judgment.

4. Luke was a traveler

The word he uses to describe his "investigations" in Luke 1:3 implies that he traveled in order to carry them out. The so-called "we-sections" in Acts indicate that he traveled with the apostle Paul on at least three occasions. (The "we-sections" are points in the story where "they" is replaced by "we," indicating Luke's presence.)

Luke's experience as a traveler is surely confirmed by his remarkable accuracy in using the correct technical seafaring terms in his dramatic description of the shipwreck in Acts 27. His accuracy in this respect was noted as long ago as 1848 by James Smith, a Scot and Fellow of the Royal Society. In *The Voyage and Shipwreck of St Paul,* Smith, writing as a yachtsman and historian, confirmed Luke's detailed references to winds, geography, and ship construction.

This interest in traveling is reflected in the story itself. Both the Gospel and the Acts are based around journeys: first that of Jesus to Jerusalem, as we saw above; second that of Paul (or more accurately of the gospel) to Rome. In both cases the account of the journey lasts for many chapters, and involves many incidental events and even diversions. But in both cases the goal is reached, because it is God's plan that it should be.

Such is the man whom the Holy Spirit was preparing to contribute more than a quarter of the whole New Testament. He was a man of the world—of the extensive Graeco-Roman world of his day. His Gentile background, his professional experience, his literary and historical gifts, his travels, and his association with Paul all made him the man for the job. His natural love for the afflicted had led him into medicine. His wide experience enabled him to see the gospel in its world setting. Paul's influence must have filled his mind with the message of free salvation offered to all irrespective of race or privilege. Luke was the man chosen and fitted by the Holy Spirit to lay emphasis on the universality of the gospel. We will now examine some of Luke's chief interests and themes, before briefly surveying both his volumes.

Luke's Special Themes

As we survey these, we will notice how the theme of the universal relevance of the gospel runs through them all.

1. The Holy Spirit

Scholars have underlined the importance of this theme for Luke. The other Gospels do not ignore it, but from the start Luke signals his special interest by emphasizing the Spirit's agency in Jesus' conception (1:35), and his inspiring Elizabeth (1:41), Zechariah (1:67), and Simeon (2:25-27) to speak words of prophecy about Jesus' birth. All the Gospels report the descent of the Spirit on to Jesus at his baptism, but Luke adds two further references to the Spirit's empowering Jesus at the start of his ministry (4:1, 14), and then crowns these by recording Jesus' dramatic claim that Isaiah 61:1 has now been fulfilled in himself: "The Spirit of the Lord is on me, because he has anointed me . . ." (Luke 4:18).

One of Luke's distinctive emphases in his portrait of our Lord is thus that his ministry is undertaken by the power of the Holy Spirit. And this is Luke's message about the church, also. Just as his Gospel begins with the outpouring of the Spirit upon Jesus at his baptism, so Acts begins with a parallel outpouring upon the church, at Pentecost. Luke then tells the story of the spread of the gospel with repeated references to the Holy Spirit (fifty-nine in all), who inspires preaching (Acts 4:8), gives boldness (4:31), directs missionary enterprise (13:2–4), gives supernatural insight (13:9–11), guides decision-making (15:28; 16:6–7; 20:22), reveals the future (20:23; 21:11), and gives encouragement (9:31) and joy (13:52) to the church. Several scholars have commented that the Acts of the Apostles might be better named the *Acts of the Holy Spirit.*

However, this would not be strictly accurate. Remarkably, Luke portrays the Spirit as the gift, not of God, but of Christ: in his Pentecost sermon Peter says of Jesus, "Exalted to the right hand of God, he has received from the Father the promised Holy Spirit and has poured out what you now see and hear" (2:33). This fits with Luke's ascription to Theophilus at the beginning of Acts: "In my former book, Theophilus, I wrote about all that Jesus began to do and to teach, until the day he was taken up to heaven" (Acts 1:1). This implies that Acts will continue the account of *Jesus'* doings and teaching. So when Luke portrays the Spirit as guiding and empowering the church, we will misunderstand him unless we link the Spirit's activity closely with that of the ascended Christ. He is "the Spirit of Jesus" (Acts 16:7), acting on behalf of the Lord of the church.

The Holy Spirit is given indiscriminately to all who believe. The prophecy fulfilled at Pentecost—"I will pour out my Spirit on all people" (Joel 2:28)—had been renewed and repeated as Jesus' ministry began: "All mankind shall see God's salvation" (Luke 3:6). These references to the inclusion of "all people" and "all mankind" within the offer of salvation stand like signposts at the beginning of each of Luke's volumes.

Contemporary Jewish belief was that the gift of the Holy Spirit was rare and special. So, for both Jews and Gentiles, the universal outpouring of the Spirit was dramatic and wonderful news—indeed, a turning-point in history, something not seen since the world was new. Luke makes this point cleverly by the long genealogy at the beginning of his Gospel (3:23–38): Jesus' ancestry is traced not just to Abraham, the father of the Jewish family (as in Matthew's Gospel), but to Adam, the founder of the human race.

2. Concern for people on the margins

Luke loves to show Jesus' concern for various groups and types of people who were on the fringes of society, or regarded as unimportant or even unclean. God's love reaches out to such people through the gospel. We may point to four such groups:

a. Women

Women had little social status in the Roman Empire, and in contemporary Jewish thought they were equally degraded. One of the daily Rabbinic thanksgivings was: "Blessed art thou, O Lord God, who hast not made me a slave, a Gentile, or a woman." Scribes and Pharisees would avoid talking to women in public, and many of them held that women were incapable of studying the Scriptures correctly.

Very different was the Christian attitude. Already, in his letter to the Galatians, Paul had made the tremendous statement, "There is neither . . . male nor female, for you are all one in Christ Jesus" (Galatians 3:28). Luke may have been influenced by Paul, but his views were doubtless formed from his knowledge of Jesus' attitude. Luke's is the Gospel of women, and more clearly than the other

Gospels it describes the open, welcoming attitude of Jesus towards women, and the place he allowed them to occupy in his ministry.

Luke makes his own point by the prominence he gives to the women in the birth stories. It is he who tells, with such delicate reserve, the story of the miraculous conception and birth of Jesus. Mary, the mother of Jesus, and Elizabeth, the mother of the Baptist, were kinswomen, and the story must have been derived directly, or indirectly, from Mary herself. Pointedly, the Holy Spirit makes his reappearance on the human scene by inspiring a woman to prophesy (1:41f.).

b. The sick

The healing work of Jesus was such a prominent feature of his ministry that all the evangelists lay great emphasis on it, but Luke more than the others. His professional interest as a doctor may be reflected here. Clearly this tender-hearted man felt the compassion of Jesus towards suffering humanity. Miracles of healing recorded only by Luke include:

- the widow of Nain's son (7:11–17)
- the crippled woman healed in the synagogue on the Sabbath (13:10–17)
- the man with dropsy (14:1–4)
- the ten lepers (17:11–19)
- the restoration of Malchus' ear, severed by the sword of Peter (22:50f.).

In Acts, the healing ministry of Jesus continues, carried on now through the hands of the apostles:

- Peter and John heal the cripple at the Beautiful Gate of the Temple, "in the name of Jesus Christ of Nazareth" (3:1–4:22).

- Philip heals many sufferers in Samaria, bringing great joy to the city (8:4–8).
- Peter cures Aeneas at Lydda with the confident words: "Aeneas, . . . Jesus Christ heals you. Get up and take care of your mat" (9:32–35), and then raises Tabitha from death in Joppa (9:36–42).

So active is the Lord's healing grace that it is said to have operated even through Peter's shadow in Jerusalem (5:15f.), and through Paul's handkerchief in Ephesus (19:11f.). In addition, a string of individual healings are ascribed to Paul:

- In Lystra he heals a poor cripple who had never walked (14:8–10).
- In Philippi he frees a slave-girl from demon-possession (16:16–18).
- In Troas he restores Eutychus to life, following the deadly effect of one of his own sermons (20:7–12)!
- In Malta he restores Publius' father to health, and then many other sick people also.

For Luke such healings are clearly part and parcel of the proclamation of the gospel. But it is interesting to note the role they play in the story. They often serve simply to gather a crowd, who then have the gospel preached to them. This reflects the "manifesto" quotation of Isaiah 61:1–2 with which Jesus' ministry begins in Luke, where "to preach the good news to the poor" is set alongside "proclaim . . . recovery of sight for the blind" (Luke 1:18). The miracles of healing are not an end in themselves, but serve the greater purpose of enabling the gospel to be heard and believed.

c. The unclean

Luke takes great delight in Jesus' boundary-breaking ministry to those who were regarded as "sinners" or "unclean." Generally speaking, Jews kept such people at arm's length, for fear of contracting their ritual "uncleanness." But Jesus reached out toward them with forgiveness and acceptance.

Leprosy sufferers are a case in point. Luke reveals a special sympathy for them. One rabbi even used to throw stones at them to make them keep their distance, but Jesus "reached out his hand and touched the leper who came to him" (Luke 5:13). Instead of contracting uncleanness from him, Jesus was able to say authoritatively, "Be clean!"

Luke alone mentions that this man was "*covered* with leprosy" (5:12). In addition, he alone records the healing of the ten men with leprosy (17:11-19), one of whom is a Samaritan and therefore doubly unclean.

In fact Samaritans are another special concern of Luke's in this category. He alone records the parable of the Good Samaritan (10:25-37). The point of this parable is not just the basic lesson that we should help those in need: far more than this, it teaches a dramatic lesson about purity and impurity. The priest and the Levite would not touch the robbers' victim, for fear of contracting impurity from a corpse. Because he does not care about such ritual matters, the Samaritan alone is able to fulfill the law of love which promises eternal life.

Luke alone records Jesus' forgiving response toward the Samaritans' customary hostility (Luke 9:52-56), and in Acts Luke lays emphasis on the advance of the gospel into Samaria, where the apostles lay hands on the "unclean" but believing Samaritans, and the Holy Spirit is poured out upon them (Acts 8:14-17).

"Now the tax collectors and 'sinners' were all gathering around to hear him. But the Pharisees and teachers of the law muttered, 'This man welcomes sinners and eats with them'" (Luke

15:1–2). So begins the famous chapter which includes the three parables of the lost, two of which (the coin and the son) are recorded only by Luke. By these three stories Jesus claims that God himself reaches out to the lost, represented by the crowd of disreputables who gather around him.

Luke's comparison of God with a shepherd, in the parable of the Lost Sheep, is dramatic indeed, for shepherds were regarded with great suspicion by the strict "Pharisees and teachers of the law" who mutter about Jesus' behavior here. Because of their nomadic lifestyle, and the inevitability of working on the Sabbath in order to keep their flocks, shepherds were classed as hopeless "sinners." But Luke has already made the heavenly choir sing the first news of the Savior's birth to an outcast group of shepherds (Luke 2:10–14): "Today in the town of David a savior has been born to *you*. . . ." So now Jesus reveals that the focus of his ministry is to draw such people back to God in repentance and faith.

While many such "sinners" would have been poor, they rub shoulders in that crowd with wealthy "tax collectors." For all their wealth, such people were still outcasts. They were customs officials, directly or indirectly employed by the hated Romans, and therefore regarded by many as "unclean" because of their contact with Gentiles, and feared by all because they made a good living out of whatever extra money they could extort from their unfortunate victims.

But God loves them—this is Luke's message. John the Baptist preaches to them (3:12f.). Jesus calls one to join his disciples (5:27f.). And when criticized for eating with this new disciple, Levi, and a crowd of his business associates, Jesus responds with his famous saying, "It is not the healthy who need a doctor, but the sick. I have not come to call the righteous, but sinners to repentance" (5:27–32).

And Luke alone records the story of another tax collector, diminutive Zacchaeus, who welcomes Jesus into his home and his heart, and prompts from Jesus the response, "Today salvation has come to this house, . . . For the Son of Man came to seek and to save what was lost" (19:9–10).

Similarly Luke alone records the parable of the Pharisee and the tax collector who go into the Temple to pray (18:9–14). The conclusion that the tax collector rather than the Pharisee "went home justified before God" must have shocked Jesus' hearers to the core. It is these unwanted sinners who are to be invited into the Kingdom, just as the man who gives a great banquet sends his servant to bring "the poor, the crippled, the blind and the lame" into the feast from which the ungrateful guests have been excluded (14:15–24).

Two further stories, both of them only in Luke, illustrate his constant concern with God's grace to sinners. The first is the story of the prostitute who comes silently behind Jesus as he reclines at table in the house of Simon the Pharisee. The feet-washing which his host has not supplied, she gives—with her tears. She also anoints Jesus' feet with ointment and covers them with kisses. He does not shrink from her. She has been forgiven. So in return she loves him much, unlike Simon (7:36–50).

The other incident takes place at the end. Matthew and Mark give us the bare information that two criminals are crucified with Jesus, one on each side of him, and that they join in the chorus of abuse which the scribes and elders are hurling at him. But Luke adds the conversation which then takes place between one of them and the Savior. For all his abuse, the criminal has some glimmering faith in the kingship of Jesus, and so he receives the promise: "Today you will be with me in paradise" (23:39–43).

d. The rich and the poor

Luke displays an even-handed concern for people at both poles of the economic spectrum. In fact the issue of money, and the problems it causes for discipleship, are a prominent interest in both his volumes.

Some of the disciples of Jesus were wealthy (for example, Zacchaeus, and Joseph of Arimathea), as were some of those who responded in Paul's missions (for example, Lydia), but the majority were poor. Jesus fulfills the prophecy which he reads in the Nazareth synagogue: he preaches the good news to the poor (Luke 4:18; 7:22), and promises them the Kingdom of God (6:20). He tells his disciples to "give up everything" in order to follow him (14:33). And in Acts we see this put into practice, as many of the first believers pool their resources into a common fund to care for the poor among them (Acts 2:44f.; 4:34f.).

In common with Matthew and Mark, Luke believed that it was very difficult, if not impossible, for a rich person to enter the Kingdom of God (Matthew 19:24; Mark 10:25; Luke 18:25). But he develops this theme of the danger of riches more than the other evangelists.

3. Prayer

Luke's special interest in prayer is a fascinating feature of both his volumes. Undoubtedly he was a person of deep prayer himself, and this is reflected in his repeated references to it—both as a feature of Jesus' life, and as a vital factor in the mission and growth of the early church.

In the Gospel there are no fewer than eleven points at which Luke adds a reference to prayer to stories he relates in parallel to Matthew and Mark:

- *3:21:* Jesus is praying as the Spirit descends upon him at his baptism.
- *5:16:* Jesus retreats into the desert to pray.
- *6:12:* Jesus prays all night before choosing the twelve apostles.
- *9:18:* Jesus prays alone before making the first prediction of his coming death and resurrection.

- *9:28f.:* Jesus goes up the mount of Transfiguration in order to pray, and is actually praying when he is transfigured.
- *11:1:* it is the sight of Jesus praying which prompts the disciples to ask, "Lord, teach us to pray," and leads to his giving the Lord's Prayer.
- *22:32:* in predicting that Peter will betray him, Jesus nonetheless assures Peter, "I have prayed for you, Simon, that your faith may not fail."
- *22:40:* in the Garden of Gethsemane, Jesus tells his disciples to "pray that you will not fall into temptation."
- *22:44f.:* Luke adds the detail that Jesus "being in anguish . . . prayed more earnestly," and then "rose from prayer" to return to his disciples.
- *23:34:* Luke alone records Jesus' prayer from the cross, "Father, forgive them, for they do not know what they are doing."
- *23:46:* "Father, into your hands I commit my spirit," is only in Luke.

We are able to look into Luke's mind as we notice this remarkable chain of references. He presents Jesus as one who was constantly at prayer, and whose whole ministry was shaped and guided by a deep awareness of inner communion with God his Father.

This emphasis continues through Luke's second volume. Prayer is one of the four pillars of the church's life (2:42), the source of power and boldness when facing opposition (4:23–31). Wonderful things happen in the context of prayer (not necessarily in answer to it: 3:1; 10:30; 12:5; 16:25). At several crucial points specific guidance is given through prayer (9:11; 10:9–16; 13:2f.), and prayer marks notable events in the life of the church (14:23; 21:5), especially healings (9:40; 28:8). For Luke, a church which does not pray is no true church.

4. *The plan and will of God*

Another vital feature of Luke's message is his deep conviction that
the story he is telling has not just "happened." It is actually the story
of how God's plan has come to pass on earth. This fulfillment of
God's plan does not override human responsibility, of course. Jesus
himself prays, "Not my will, but yours be done," and then receives
extra strength to do the will of God before him (22:42f.). Similarly
Paul has to commit himself with determination to do God's will as
he too approaches death in Jerusalem, and others try to persuade
him not to go there (Acts 21:12–14). God's plan is also opposed by
those who resist him. But, in spite of all the opposition and through
all the complexities of human response, God's will is done.

This theme in Luke has been studied by John Squires, who
notes five ways in which Luke underlines this theme:

a. God is in charge of history

From creation (Luke 3:38) through to final judgment (Acts 17:31),
he is in charge. This point is subtly made in Luke 2:1, where the
mind of the Roman emperor is moved to issue a decree which will
bring a young peasant girl from Nazareth to Bethlehem so that her
baby, the son of David, will be born in David's town.

b. God is in charge of the church

He directs both the Lord Jesus, and the church, in the course
their ministry should take. Luke quietly makes this point by his
repeated use of a little Greek word often translated "it is necessary. . . ." He uses this phrase on no fewer than forty-two occasions
in his two volumes. If we ask, *Why* is it "necessary"?, the answer
usually is, because that is what God has planned.

c. God directly intervenes to steer events

This occurs on several occasions, especially in Acts: for instance, on three occasions an angel appears to Paul, each time giving him guidance about the next stage of his mission (Acts 16:9f.; 23:11; 27:23f.). Healings are also the direct action of God, enabling the gospel to spread.

d. Scripture has been fulfilled, supremely in Jesus but also in the life of the church

Luke constantly brings the fulfillment of prophecy to our attention, and this underlines the accomplishment of God's plan. He makes this point forcibly in the story of Jesus' appearance on the road to Emmaus (Luke 24:13–35). A personal revelation of himself would have healed the agony of the two disciples, but Jesus deliberately postpones this until he has shown them that both the death and the resurrection of the Christ were foretold by Scripture (24:25–27, 46f.).

e. God has foreordained certain vital events

These take place, whatever the opposition. Peter in his Pentecost sermon charges his hearers with brutally murdering Jesus, but adds the comment, "This man was handed over to you by God's set purpose and foreknowledge" (Acts 2:23). Similarly, in their prayer when facing the first persecution, the Jerusalem believers see God's plan behind the crucifixion: "They did what your power and will had decided beforehand should happen" (Acts 4:28).

It is hard to define the relationship between this sovereignty of God and the responsibility of the human agents involved—both those who oppose his plan, and those who obey it. All we can say is that Luke did not feel any conflict between the two ideas. The result is a powerful confidence: whatever problems may beset the church, however tortuous events may seem, however powerful the enemies of the gospel may be, God will bring about the fulfillment of his plan. So, through many hardships, the gospel reaches Rome, the center of the empire, and the story ends with open proclamation there (Acts 28:30f.).

Scholars have puzzled about the end of Acts. It seems to finish abruptly, and we never discover the outcome of the appeal to the emperor which has brought Paul to Rome. It may be that his trial had not yet taken place when Luke finished writing. But in any case, the abrupt ending gives the impression of a story not yet finished, and enables us to link our experience on to that of the apostles, and thus to have the same confidence that whatever the hardships and setbacks we may experience, the gospel will triumph for us too.

Luke's Two Volumes

Finally we will survey the Gospel and Acts, to draw out some of the ways in which Luke has structured the story and conveys his message.

1. The Gospel

a. Birth and preparation, 1:1–4:13

After the preface, Luke's Gospel begins in a thoroughly Jewish atmosphere. The scene is set in the Temple at Jerusalem, and the first figure to whom we are introduced is a priest married to one of the daughters of Aaron. The son promised to this pious couple is to keep the ancient Nazirites' vow from his birth

(1:15). He will be a prophet, speaking "in the spirit and power of Elijah" (1:17).

The Jewish and Old Testament atmosphere continues through the promise of the Messiah to Mary, the story of his birth, and the songs which she, Zechariah, and Simeon all sing (1:46–55, 67–79; 2:29–32). This atmosphere is not accidental. Though writing for Gentile readers, Luke does not mean to suggest that Christianity is a new religion with no historical roots in the past. What has happened is a fulfillment of God's covenant with Abraham and of his promises through the prophets (1:54–55, 70, 72f.). But the fulfillment is richer than the expectation, and from the throne of David he will be seen to reign over the whole world, not just over Israel.

This wider perspective appears in 2:1, with the reference to the current occupant of the world throne, Caesar Augustus. He has no idea what God is planning and bringing about in a distant corner of his empire—through a poor peasant family, supported by a group of shepherds. This world context is further emphasized by the song of the angels (2:14), and by the way Luke introduces the ministry of John the Baptist (3:1–2). These chapters are concerned with preparations for the ministry of the new King: his own growth (2:41–52); the preaching of John the Baptist (3:1–22); his hidden ancestry which makes him a turning-point in world history (3:23–38); and his defeat of the Devil in the power of the Spirit (4:1–13).

b. The ministry in Galilee, 4:14–9:50

This first main section of the Gospel begins with the remarkable account of Jesus' visit to Nazareth (4:16–30). Matthew and Mark describe a similar incident toward the end of the ministry in Galilee (Matthew 13:53–58; Mark 6:1–6), and it is unclear whether Luke is recounting a different visit, or whether he has deliberately altered the sequence of events in order to begin his account of Jesus' ministry with this powerful story.

In any case, the meaning of the incident to Luke is clear. It introduces Jesus' ministry in three ways: firstly, the quotation of Isaiah 61:1–2 stands like a motto at the head of the story. We will see Jesus doing all these things—preaching, healing, even proclaiming release in the case of Barabbas (23:25) who represents all who find undeserved freedom through Jesus.

Secondly, it foreshadows his final rejection by the Jewish people. It is a somber story indeed: anointed by the Spirit, he is spurned by his people.

And thirdly, it underlines the universal mission he will launch. The audience is outraged by Jesus' reference to Naaman and to the widow of Zarephath, who were foreigners blessed by God in preference to Israelites in equal need (4:25–27). At the opposite end of the story, Paul makes an identical point to the Jews of Rome who similarly reject the gospel he preaches: "Therefore I want you to know that God's salvation has been sent to the Gentiles, and they will listen!" (Acts 28:28). This mission to the Gentiles was entailed right from the start by Jesus, even though he himself focused on Israel.

So during the Galilean ministry Jesus particularly reveals his love for the Gentile stranger. The Roman centurion's servant is healed (7:1–10). Luke gives a longer version of this story than Matthew, recording the centurion's humility ("I did not even consider myself worthy to come to you" [verse 7]), and showing the concern of the Jewish elders for this Gentile.

c. Jesus travels to Jerusalem, 9:51–19:40

Many scholars regard 9:51 as the turning-point of the Gospel. Jesus now leaves Galilee and starts journeying towards Jerusalem. One writer, David Gooding, describes 1:1–9:50 as the "Coming" of

Jesus from heaven to earth, culminating in the revelation of glory at the transfiguration. The second half of the Gospel, from 9:51 onwards, is correspondingly the "Going" of Jesus from earth to heaven, likewise culminating in glory, the glory of the ascension.

This long section of the Gospel is composed almost exclusively of material not found in Mark, much of it unique to Luke, and has been called Luke's "Travel Narrative." Jesus gradually moves toward the final rejection in Jerusalem, toward suffering which we realize is central to his mission, and in incident after incident we discover more about what it means to follow him. Discipleship means being on the move, with him, leaving behind security and home (9:57-62) for a life of faith, prayer, obedience, and sacrifice in reaching out to those in need.

d. Jesus in Jerusalem, 19:41–24:53

At the beginning of this final section Jesus enters Jerusalem with great sorrow because he knows the city will reject him, and he foresees dreadful judgment (19:41-44). The section ends, in contrast, with the disciples entering Jerusalem "with great joy" (24:52) because this rejection of Jesus by Israel means that the Scriptures have been fulfilled, the Holy Spirit has been promised, and all nations will now hear the Good News of repentance and forgiveness (24:45-49).

In between these two "entries" we discover how the one event—the crucifixion of Jesus—can be two such very different things, both a horrible rejection and dreadful crime, and a fulfillment of God's plan for the salvation of the world. It is simply a matter of looking at the event from two very different perspectives. Luke thus challenges his Gentile readers: how will they regard it? Like Pilate, as a petty religious squabble of little consequence? Or like the disciples and Luke himself, as the fulfillment of God's plan to destroy death for all mankind?

2. The Acts

Volume two begins exactly where volume one ends. The disciples are in Jerusalem, waiting for the Holy Spirit to be given (1:5). A brief introduction summarizes the period before the ascension, and sets the agenda for the next stage: "You will receive power when the Holy Spirit comes on you; and you will be my witnesses in Jerusalem, and in all Judea and Samaria, and to the ends of the earth" (1:8).

This picture of concentric geographical circles forms the structure of Acts. As far as the end of chapter 7, the action is set in Jerusalem. But with the death of Stephen, ". . . a great persecution broke out against the church at Jerusalem, and all except the apostles were scattered throughout Judea and Samaria" (8:1). The circle widens.

Judea and Samaria remain the scene of operations as far as 9:31, which is one of Luke's little summaries of "the story so far": "Then the church throughout Judea, Galilee, and Samaria enjoyed a time of peace. It was strengthened; and encouraged by the Holy Spirit, it grew in numbers, living in the fear of the Lord."

But the seeds of further development have already been sown. We have traveled to Syria, to witness the conversion of Saul in Damascus (9:1–19), and have heard the Lord's word to him through Ananias, "This man is my chosen instrument to carry my name before the Gentiles and their kings and before the people of Israel" (9:15).

Now these seeds begin to germinate. Even though, geographically, the action remains basically within Judea and Samaria for the next three chapters, the story of the conversion of Cornelius in chapter 10 prepares us for the explosion which takes place at the beginning of chapter 13. Here Paul and Barnabas are sent out by the Holy Spirit into the Gentile world, and in three successive missionary journeys we see the gospel growing gradually further from Jerusalem and closer to "the ends of the earth" (1:8).

a. Jerusalem foundations, 1:9–7:60

The Day of Pentecost supplies an initial fulfillment of the vision of Acts 1:8. The gift of tongues enables the disciples to speak in the native language of all the visitors to Jerusalem. As Professor Howard Marshall has pointed out, this gift was not necessary in order actually to communicate with those present. Undoubtedly, the vast majority of them were able to speak koinē Greek. So the significance of the event was that they heard "the wonders of God" (2:11) in the dialects of their pagan, non-Jewish neighbors. They, too, are those for whom this message is designed.

Peter draws out this significance of the event. He explains that it is a fulfillment of God's promise to pour out his Spirit upon all flesh (2:17f.), not only upon all nations, but upon both sexes ("sons and daughters"), old and young ("young men . . . old men"), and all ranks of society (even "servants, both men and women"). In fact, as Peter goes on to say, still quoting from Joel, "everyone who calls on the name of the Lord will be saved" (2:21). In his final appeal he makes it clear that the promise is not only "for you and your children" but also "for all who are far off" (2:39), which is a phrase describing the Gentiles. God has kept his covenant with Abraham to bless all the families of the earth through his offspring (3:25; Genesis 12:3).

In chapters 3–7 the church in Jerusalem is built up. Nothing can stop the word of God. There are problems: persecution (4:1–31; 5:17–42), hypocrisy (5:1–11), and disunity (6:1–7). But through all these "the word of God spread" (6:7). In 2:41, there are 3,000 believers; in 4:4, 5,000; in 5:14, there are "more and more men and women;" and in 6:7, "the number of disciples in Jerusalem increased rapidly."

This section reaches a climax with the defense and martyrdom of Stephen (6:8–8:1). He is accused of speaking against Moses (6:11), saying that Jesus will destroy the Temple and change the law (6:13–14). The charge is serious. Stephen's eloquent and able defense makes clear what he had in fact been teaching; and Luke uses his long record of Stephen's speech (7:2–53) to prepare his readers for the next turns the story will take.

In a nutshell, Stephen says that the old particularism has given way to a new universalism. God is not tied to a building, or to one country. He was with Abraham in Mesopotamia and Haran and Palestine; with Joseph in Egypt; with Moses in the land of Midian; with the Israelites in the wilderness; with Joshua as he settled the nation in the promised land. True, Solomon built the Temple, but the prophet Isaiah said that God's throne was in heaven and that the earth was his footstool. The evidence of the Old Testament is clear, that "the Most High does not live in houses made by men" (7:48).

The importance of Stephen's speech and death is threefold. Theologically, it paves the way for the coming mission to the Gentiles. Personally, it leads into the conversion of Saul, who participated in Stephen's murder, and who no doubt had heard his speech. He will become the greatest exponent of Stephen's gospel! And geographically, as we have seen, Stephen's death leads to the expansion of the gospel from Jerusalem into Judea and Samaria (8:1).

b. The pressure builds, 8:1–12:25

This whole section may be pictured by thinking of a water-boiler in which the pressure gradually rises until the rivets cannot stand the strain any longer and the inevitable happens—an explosion. The explosion occurs at the beginning of chapter 13, when finally the gospel bursts out into the Gentile world, under the powerful impetus of the Spirit.

The pressure begins to build with the expansion into Samaria in chapter 8, also marked by special activity of the Holy Spirit. The conversion of Saul adds to it, and then the long episode in which

Peter's vision and experience with Cornelius are related *twice* accelerates the buildup. How can the church resist the leading of the Holy Spirit, who is evidently breaking down the old barrier between Jews and Gentiles? The multiracial church in Antioch comes into being, but not with the whole hearted support of the Jerusalem church (11:20f.). In chapter 12 it all seems to stall. Yet "the word of God continued to increase and spread" (12:24). How long can the pressure continue to increase before the boiler will burst?

c. Paul's first missionary journey, 13:1–15:35

Once again the Spirit steps in and pushes the church forward. It may seem natural to us that people can be Christians without also being Jews, but this was by no means obvious to the first believers. Like Paul and Barnabas on their first missionary venture, they discover by experience that, when Jews rejected the gospel, "the Gentiles . . . were glad and honored the word of the Lord; and all who were appointed for eternal life believed" (13:48). The Holy Spirit seems to demand only that they believe in the Lord Jesus. They are not required to become Jews as well. At the end of their missionary tour, Paul and Barnabas gladly conclude that God has simply "opened the door of faith to the Gentiles" (14:27).

But some believe that the action of the Holy Spirit needs careful interpretation. A delegation arrives in Antioch, insisting that "Unless you are circumcised, according to the custom taught by Moses, you cannot be saved" (15:1). So the episode which Luke describes in Acts 15 is a vital consequence of the mission just completed. Paul and Barnabas are appointed, with others, to go up to Jerusalem to settle the matter with "the apostles and elders" (Acts 15:4): must Gentiles also become Jews in order to be saved?

It is likely that around this time Paul wrote his letter to the Galatians as a circular sent to the churches which he had founded on his missionary journey. The letter is a passionate defense of the view which also prevailed at the Jerusalem conference—that our "justification," or acceptance before God, depends not on our obedience to the law, but solely on Christ, to whom we are united by faith.

With this vital issue decided, the foundation is laid for the gospel to spread without hindrance "to the ends of the earth."

d. Paul's second missionary journey, 15:36–18:22

This begins as a project to revisit the churches founded on the first journey (15:36), but once again the Holy Spirit steps in and directs them further. Before long, Paul and his companions are deciding that they should cross into Greece with the gospel (16:10), and they end up ministering successively in Philippi, Thessalonica, Berea, Athens, and Corinth. Paul stays over eighteen months in Corinth before finally returning to his "home" church in Antioch.

e. Paul's third missionary journey, 18:23–21:16

It looks as though Paul had conceived the idea of making Ephesus a center of ministry, similar to Corinth (18:21). This he now does, spending over two years there. Ephesus was, like Antioch, one of the largest cities in the empire and the focus of the life of a large surrounding area. But once again the Spirit steps in and shapes Paul's mind about his strategy: Rome! The rather tortuous route on which Paul decides (19:21) is probably shaped by the collection he has been making for the church in Jerusalem (for example, Romans 15:25–27): he wants to take it there personally.

Paul is clearly concerned about the visit to Jerusalem. He asks the Romans to pray "that I may be rescued from the unbelievers in Judea and that my service in Jerusalem may be acceptable to the saints there" (Romans 15:31). Luke underlines this sense of foreboding by reporting the prophetic messages which point to coming imprisonment (20:22f.; 21:10–14). And sure enough, when Paul arrives in Jerusalem he rapidly gets into trouble with the Jews and Jewish Christians who disapprove deeply of his law-free gospel.

f. The journey to Rome, 21:17–28:31

These final chapters of Acts contain some of the most gripping writing in the whole Bible. The remarkable thing is that, from the moment at which Paul is seized by the rioting crowd in Acts 21:30, he never regains his freedom. He spends the rest of the book a prisoner, apparently helpless before the vagaries of Roman justice.

But the way in which Luke tells the story gives a totally different impression. Paul is not bound and helpless. God's plan is being worked out. Paul has opportunities to witness to a vast crowd in Jerusalem, to the Jewish Sanhedrin, to two Roman governors, to King Herod and his wife, to a ship's company of nearly 300, to the Governor of Malta and through him to many other islanders, to the leaders of the vast Jewish community in Rome, and finally to all who want to come and hear him in the imperial capital. Paul may have been a prisoner, but as he puts it later to Timothy, "God's word is not chained!" (2 Timothy 2:9).

Luke's message is thus finally a great encouragement to a suffering and weak church. Under whatever difficulties it labors, and however powerless it may seem, the church will always be led in a "triumphal procession" (2 Corinthians 2:14) if we follow the example of Paul, trust in the Lord of the church, and seize the opportunities he gives.

CHAPTER 4

John and His Message

Jesus did many other miraculous signs in the presence of his disciples, which are not recorded in this book. But these are written that you may believe that Jesus is the Christ, the Son of God, and that by believing you may have life in his name.

(John 20:30–31)

There are five separate documents in our New Testament which are attributed to John, namely, the Gospel bearing his name, the three letters, and the book of Revelation. Of these, Revelation is so different in subject matter that it must receive separate treatment, whether or not it was written by the same John.

It is widely agreed, however, that the Gospel and the letters come from the pen of the same author. Not only is the Greek style very similar, but there are many striking theological phrases which are prominent in both—phrases such as "Spirit of truth," "light" and "darkness," "of the world," "children of God," "born of God," "abiding in" Christ, "keeping his commandments," "love," "witness," "life," and "death."

John the Man and His Gospel

But who was the author? This is a complicated and controversial question. The traditional view is that the Gospel and letters were written in his old age at Ephesus by the apostle John the son of Zebedee. This view goes back as far as Irenaeus, Bishop of Lyons from 178 until his death in *c.* AD 195. Irenaeus claimed to have a direct link with John through Polycarp, the Bishop of Smyrna martyred in AD 156 at the age of eighty-six. In a famous letter preserved by Eusebius, the church historian, Irenaeus tells a friend how, as a young man, he sat at Polycarp's feet and heard him describe his conversations with John and the teaching he had received directly from the apostle. We can well imagine Polycarp, at the age of twenty, listening to the apostle John, who would by then himself have been in his eighties, and there seems little reason to question Irenaeus' claim.

When Irenaeus asserts, therefore, that John the son of Zebedee wrote the Fourth Gospel, and that he was the unnamed "disciple whom Jesus loved" who reclined next to Jesus at the last supper (13:23), we must take his testimony seriously.

It has to be said, however, that only a handful of critical scholars have accepted this evidence. Their reluctance arises from the view, shared by the majority of scholars, that John's Gospel is not fundamentally a historical work at all. Rather, it is the result of a long process of theological development, and so reflects the thought of a later period dressed up in Gospel form.

Some scholars have added a particular twist to this view, arguing that the Gospel reflects the history and experiences, not of Jesus and his disciples, but of a particular church to which the evangelist (not John) belonged. For the encouragement of his church, this evangelist wrote the story of Jesus as if he had been through the same experiences of rejection and persecution as they.

This lack of respect for John's Gospel as history results from three features of it which do indeed require explanation:

1. In many respects John presents a different picture of Jesus from that in the synoptic Gospels. For instance, in John's Gospel Jesus is not in the least reticent about claiming to be the Son of God in public (e.g. 5:19–30).
2. There is no difference in style between the teaching of Jesus in John and the evangelist's own words. This suggests that the evangelist is responsible for the language of the discourses in which Jesus speaks.
3. The Gospel is beautifully constructed. Scholars are prepared to agree that it is a literary masterpiece. But many feel that an author who devoted such care to the structure and composition of his work cannot also have been concerned to report history.

Taken together, these three points are held by a majority of scholars to make it impossible that the Gospel was written by an eyewitness of the ministry of Jesus. And therefore the early church fathers' external ascription to John, the son of Zebedee, is set aside on internal grounds.

However, we must seriously question this scholarly consensus.

1. John and the synoptics

The undoubted differences between John's Gospel and the synoptics do not necessarily mean that John is historically unreliable. These differences were noticed in the early church, and lie behind Clement of Alexandria's comment (*c.* AD 200) that "last of all John, knowing that the 'bodily' facts had been made clear in the other Gospels, composed a 'spiritual' Gospel, urged on by the other disciples and inspired by the Spirit."

Clement's description of John as a "spiritual" Gospel has often been quoted in support of the view that John was not interested in history. But nothing could be further from the truth. According to

Clement, John was concerned to convey the inner essence of Jesus, the "spirit" within the "body," and thus to provide an account which could claim to be just as historically reliable as the synoptics.

In addition, it is remarkable to note the many points at which John's account supplements that of the synoptics. These points have been set out and discussed in a famous essay by Dr. Leon Morris. It is quite possible that John was deliberately employing traditions and memories which had not been utilized in the synoptic tradition.

In several respects John elaborates the picture they paint. For instance, by emphasizing Jesus' reticence about proclaiming himself as "the Christ" in public, the synoptics could prompt the accusation that people can hardly be blamed for not believing in him. But John makes it clear that the hindrance to faith did not lie on Jesus' side. Viewed from a different angle, his self-proclamation was as clear as crystal, so that the responsibility rests wholly with us, if we refuse to believe.

2. The language of John

It is true that there is no stylistic difference between the discourses in which Jesus speaks, and the narrative parts of the Gospel for which the evangelist was responsible. However, we must remember that Jesus did not teach in Greek. He spoke Aramaic, and therefore all our records of his teaching are in translation. It is well known how two translations of the same original may differ greatly from each other because the style and vocabulary of the translation are the choice of the translator.

It has long been recognized that John's Greek has many Hebrew and Aramaic features, so that the author was clearly bilingual. In addition, if it is true that John wanted to convey the inner essence of Jesus' teaching and person, it is hardly surprising if the language of the discourses reflects John's own style.

3. The structure of John's Gospel

The author himself reveals the care with which he has composed his Gospel. He describes it in terms of selectivity: "Jesus did many other miraculous signs in the presence of his disciples, which are not recorded in this book. But these are written that you may believe that Jesus is the Christ, the Son of God, and that by believing you may have life in his name" (20:30f.). As we shall see, the structure and message of the book focus on the "signs," the miraculous acts of Jesus which point beyond themselves to truths about his person. The particular "signs"—all but one of them unique to John—have been chosen to achieve a particular purpose, that of convincing the readers to believe in Jesus as "the Christ."

This means that the signs were chosen for inclusion with the particular needs of the readers in mind. The evangelist was concerned to show the relevance of the ministry of Jesus to their needs. But this in turn does not mean that the evangelist had no historical concern. On the contrary, he had no gospel of which to convince his readers if Jesus did not really perform these "signs" which show his messiahship.

There is little substance, therefore, in the reasons often given for rejecting the powerful testimony of Irenaeus. But if we assume that the author of both the Gospel and the letters is the apostle John, what can we say about him?

a. He was an eyewitness

Despite the general antipathy to the traditional ascription to John, scholars have been ready to recognize that the author shows a profound knowledge of the geography of Palestine (e.g. 1:28; 4:5f., 20), of Jerusalem (e.g. 5:2; 19:13), of the Temple before its destruction (e.g. 2:20; 8:20; 10:23), and of the general state of affairs in Israel at the time of Jesus. For instance J. Louis Martyn, a scholar who more than any other has shaped the contemporary scholarly consensus, nonetheless confesses that John's various statements about Jewish faith and life "stand proudly among the most accurate statements about Jewish thought in the whole of the New Testament."

John's accuracy in these respects must surely suggest a concern for accuracy in his record of the events of Jesus' ministry— most of which he must have directly witnessed, as one of the Twelve. His accounts are peppered with allusions to time and place, as well as with other incidental details, all of which add nothing to the story except to underline the implicit claim that the author knows his material intimately (e.g. 1:39; 2:1; 3:23; 4:6, 40; 11:54; 18:10; 21:11).

b. He had an intimate knowledge of Jesus

In 21:24 the author is identified, not by name, but as "the disciple whom Jesus loved" (compare 21:20). This "beloved disciple" is mentioned also in 13:23; 19:26; 20:2; and 21:7, and many scholars believe that he is also the anonymous "other disciple" of 18:15f. On each occasion when this disciple appears, the intimacy of his relationship with Jesus is underlined.

He first appears reclining next to Jesus in the upper room, so close to him that he can lean back and whisper to him without being overheard by the others (13:21–25; compare 21:20). Next we discover that, even though Jesus has predicted that the disciples will all abandon him (16:32), this particular disciple accompanies him into the courtyard of the High Priest's house (18:15). Jesus entrusts his mother to him from the cross (19:25–27), and he is the one (again with Peter) to whom Mary Magdalene runs with the news of the empty tomb (20:1f.). Finally, it is the beloved disciple who first recognizes the risen Lord on the Galilean shore and shouts to Peter, "It is the Lord!" (21:7), and who then shares in the private conversation which the Lord has with Peter after breakfast (21:20–23).

If this "beloved disciple" was John, we can fill out this picture of intimacy from the synoptic Gospels. Peter, James, and John together formed an inner circle within the Twelve, permitted by Jesus to witness certain crucial events. They see the raising of Jairus' daughter (Luke 8:51), witness his glory on the mount of Transfiguration (Mark 9:2), hear his apocalyptic teaching (Mark 13:3), and stay near him during his bitter agony in the garden (Mark 14:33).

Altogether, John enjoyed the most intimate possible relationship with Jesus, and so was more qualified than any other of the Twelve to convey to us the inner mind of the Lord. He had seen him with his eyes (1 John 1:1–3; compare 1 John 4:14 and John 1:14); heard him with his ears and touched him with his hands (1 John 1:1–3). He had absorbed his Lord's own mind, penetrated to the heart of his self-revelation, and truly caught the spirit of his Master.

c. He had been profoundly changed by Jesus

John and James, according to Mark, were nicknamed by Jesus "Boanerges," which means "sons of thunder" (Mark 3:17), and several incidents in the Gospel narratives reveal their stormy temperament. It is John who resents and forbids the ministry of the exorcist who was not one of the Twelve (Luke 9:49f.). It is the sons of thunder together who are offended by the refusal of a Samaritan village to receive Jesus, and who, Elijah-like, want to call down fire from heaven to consume it (Luke 9:51–56). And it is the same two brothers who come with their mother to ask that the best seats in the Kingdom might be reserved for them (Mark 10:35–45; Matthew 20:20–28).

How little they then seem to understand the spirit of Jesus! He has to rebuke them: "You do not know what kind of spirit you are of" (Luke 9:55 footnote), and again: "You don't know what you are asking" (Matthew 20:22; Mark 10:38). Yet this son of thunder has become known to us as "the apostle of love." It is clear that the warm sun of his Master's love made the thunder clouds evaporate.

Now he is more than open to the ministry of others outside the Twelve: the most effective evangelist in his Gospel is the Samaritan woman (4:39). And now he shows the Samaritans in the warmest possible light: they surpass the Jews in their believing response to Jesus (4:42), and "urge" Jesus to stay with them (4:40). And now, far from seeking recognition and status alongside the Lord, he effaces his name completely from the story, and gives himself a new name, one which records the only epitaph he desires: forget all else, I was loved by Jesus!

John was thus eminently suited to communicate the heart of his Lord. He desired to introduce his readers to the Person he had come to know and love. He wanted them to have fellowship with him, too (1 John 1:3), and he expected them to be transformed in character as he had been.

In fact, he explains clearly the purposes for which he wrote. He wrote his Gospel that his readers might believe in Jesus, and experience life through faith in him (20:31), and he wrote his first letter to those who had already believed, in order that they might know that they had life (1 John 5:13). His theology is deep and mind-stretching, but his ultimate purpose is practical. He desired his readers both to receive eternal life and to know that they had received it.

For his readers to receive eternal life they must put their trust in Jesus Christ, since life resides in him (1:4). Therefore in his Gospel John sets forth Jesus Christ in all his divine-human glory, that we might see and believe. In particular, he seems to have directed his writing at Jews, for he emphasizes the way in which Jesus fulfills and replaces all the great institutions of Judaism—the Temple, the law, the annual festivals. The Temple and its worship were lost, destroyed by the Romans, in AD 70: after this date,

John's Gospel could have had an especially powerful appeal to Jews whose mourning was turned to joy by the discovery that God had already provided for the loss through Jesus.

For his readers to know that they had received eternal life, it was necessary for them to understand clearly the indispensable marks of authentic Christianity. In his letters, particularly in his first, he therefore proceeds to set these forth, as we shall see.

The Message of John's Gospel

1. The foundations of faith

The road to life is faith (3:14–16, 36; 6:47; 20:31). But on what does faith rest? John would agree with the answer given by Paul in Romans 10:17: "Faith comes from hearing the message, and the message is heard through the word of Christ." Faith is never isolated. It is always a response to God's initiative. In particular, it is evoked by his word, or, as John would have said, by his "testimony." To believe God's testimony, given through Christ, is to take the first vital steps into a faith which will lead to eternal life: this above all is the message of John's Gospel.

At the moment it is the scholarly fashion to maintain that John does not argue for faith, but assumes it. Many scholars hold, therefore, that John's Gospel is not evangelistic, that is, not designed to convince unbelievers of the rightness of faith in Christ. But this view barely fits the evidence of the Gospel itself. John's statement of his purpose in 20:31 expresses an evangelistic intent. And in the Gospel this theme of testimony seems to be developed particularly with Jewish unbelievers in mind. What testimony does John produce?

a. Human testimony

In the opening words of the Gospel, as in those of the first letter and Revelation, John bears his own apostolic witness to the Lord Jesus Christ: "We have seen his glory" (1:14). He thus begins his Gospel with statement, not with proof. Just as Genesis is introduced by "In the beginning God," announcing the Father's existence, so John's Gospel is introduced by "In the beginning was the Word," affirming the Son's pre-existence with God.

These eternal truths are the product of divine revelation, not of human speculation. But now they are communicated by the passionate testimony of human beings who have become convinced of them. The Gospel begins and ends on this note of apostolic testimony (compare 21:24). In the intervening chapters we meet a succession of people who all encounter Jesus and bear witness to him:

- *John the Baptist's* testimony is introduced alongside John's at the start (1:6–8), and is the most elaborate (see also 1:19–36; 3:25–30; 10:40–42), perhaps because John was widely recognized as a prophet by Jews in John's day.
- *A succession of disciples* encounter Jesus and bear witness (1:37–51): Andrew convinces his brother Simon, and Philip brings Nathanael, who then makes a remarkable confession of faith (1:49).
- *The Samaritans* bear powerful testimony in chapter 4: first the woman becomes convinced that Jesus is "the Messiah" (4:29), and then her compatriots decide that Jesus is "the Savior of the world" (4:42).
- *Peter* (6:68f.), *the Jerusalem crowd* (7:40–42), *the man born blind* (9:17), *Martha* (11:27), and *Thomas* (20:28) all bear different testimony to Jesus, depending on their different experience of him. Thomas' confession forms a powerful climax to the whole story.

In his portrayal John does not hesitate to include testimony against Jesus (e.g. 7:52; 8:52f.; 9:16; 10:20), and so his readers are forced to take sides: whose testimony will they believe?

In order to decide this, evidence needs to be presented, and further witnesses summoned. Although these human witnesses are important, Jesus does not rely on their testimony to validate his claims (5:34). He even accepts the legal principle, "If I testify to myself, my testimony is not valid" (5:31). In Jewish courts, no testimony could be accepted unless it was corroborated. The Pharisees throw this at Jesus in 8:13: "Here you are, appearing as your own witness; your testimony is not valid." But Jesus accepts this point, and replies, "In your own Law it is written that the testimony of two men is valid. I am one who testifies for myself; my other witness is the Father, who sent me" (8:17f.). And so a second witness is called:

b. Divine testimony

Dr. A. E. Harvey has illuminated the significance of Jesus' calling God to witness in 5:37 and 8:18 (compare also 8:50; 10:32). In Jewish courts, solitary testimony could be acceptable if the accused solemnly called God to witness that his testimony was true. This was a serious step to take because, if he was in fact lying, the accused was thought to lay himself open to the judgment of God. And conversely, his accusers would have to think twice and three times before repeating their accusation, because they too could be opposing God and drawing his judgment upon themselves.

This is the solemn spirit in which Jesus calls God to witness on his behalf. In any case, the nature of Jesus' claim is such that only God could authenticate and support it: Jesus claims to be the Son, uniquely authorized to give life and to exercise judgment, both the prerogatives of God himself (5:19–23). So it is not only a bold move, but essential to his case, that Jesus should cite God as a witness on his behalf.

A. E. Harvey has helpfully shown, in his book *Jesus on Trial,* how the imagery of the law-court pervades the whole Gospel of John. John presents his account of Jesus' ministry as if Jesus were on trial throughout, and not just at the end before the High Priest. In fact, in this Gospel Jesus is never *formally* tried at all. He is executed without due process of law, even though he himself asks for witnesses to be called when he is brought before the High Priest (18:21). The trial occurs in this informal sense, throughout the book, so that John's readers are themselves put on the spot, and compelled to come to their own decision.

They will ask, as Jesus' opponents do, how God bears witness to his Son (e.g. 8:19). This divine testimony, John replies, is threefold:

i. *The Father speaks his testimony through the lips of Jesus.* Again and again Jesus denies that he speaks his words on his own authority. His authority is derived from the Father who is their author. Is not he himself the Word of God incarnate (1:1, 14)? Then his words are the words of God (3:34):

- "My teaching is not my own. It comes from him who sent me" (7:16).
- "I do nothing on my own but speak just what the Father has taught me" (8:28).
- "For I did not speak of my own accord, but the Father who sent me commanded me what to say and how to say it. . . . So whatever I say is just what the Father has told me to say" (12:49f.).
- "I gave them the words you gave me and they accepted them. . . . I have given them your word" (17:8, 14).

Jesus expects everyone who hears him to believe his words because they are God's words. In making this solemn claim, he is deliberately alluding to the famous promise given to Moses in

Deuteronomy 18:18: "I will raise up for them a prophet like you from among their brothers; I will put my words in his mouth, and he will tell them everything I command him."

John, of course, believes that Jesus speaks God's words not just because he is the "prophet like Moses" whom people were expecting (compare 1:21) but because he is far more than a prophet: he is the very "Word of God" in person. But as such, he fulfills the prophecy of Deuteronomy 18, and his readers need to be put on the spot: will they listen?

In this connection it is worth noting the remarkable new designation of God in John's Gospel as "he who sent me" (thirty-six times), and correspondingly of Jesus as "the one he has sent." These paraphrases for the names "Father" and "Son" nearly always occur in contexts where the Son's authority is challenged or the Father's claimed. "He who sent" vindicates the authority of "the one he has sent":

- "The one whom God has sent speaks the words of God" (3:34).
- "He who sent me is reliable, and what I have heard from him I tell the world" (8:26).
- "Jesus, still teaching in the temple courts, cried out, '. . . I am not here on my own, but he who sent me is true. You do not know him, but I know him because I am from him and he sent me'" (7:28f.).

The validity of Jesus' testimony is due to his descent from heaven (3:11–13).

ii. *The Father dramatizes his testimony in the works of Jesus.* Jesus' "works," like his "words," have been given to him by God, so that they are really God's works, a dramatic testimony to Jesus' unique sonship. Just as he can say, "My teaching is not mine. It comes from him who sent me" (7:16), so he can speak of "the very work that the Father has given me to finish" (5:36; compare 5:19–30 and 10:31–39). So the Son acts "from the Father" (10:32), and the Father acts "in the Son" (10:38; 14:10). The works are the Father's, although performed through the Son. This double testimony of words and works should have been adequate to elicit faith (14:11), and in fact many simple folk see the works (6:14), hear the words (7:40f.), and believe (11:45).

But how did his works actually speak a message about him? John's characteristic word for the miracles of Jesus is "signs," because they contain a message which faith will discern.

Nicodemus is quite right in declaring that Jesus can perform such "signs" only because God is with him: ". . . you are a teacher who has come from God" (3:2). But do they indicate something more about Jesus, beyond this rather bare insight? Nicodemus is puzzled. Some of the Jerusalem crowd think they prove that he is the Christ (7:31). But others disagree: Jesus' brothers, for example, have seen the signs and think little of them (7:3–5). Even when people "believed in his name" because of the signs, Jesus is nonetheless very cautious about the quality of their faith (2:23–25).

The fact is that the signs can only speak if they are interpreted, and that is what John aims to do. So, for instance, the healing of the lame man in 5:1–9 does not show only Jesus' wonderful power or mercy: rather, it shows his authority to tell God's people what they may do on the Sabbath, and further it reveals his unique relationship with the Father, because he displays the "works" of God himself by his action (5:9–20). Similarly, the feeding of the 5,000 (6:1–14) is then interpreted by the long following dialogue, in which Jesus proclaims himself as "the bread of life" (6:25–59). John's selection of the signs for inclusion in his Gospel (20:30f.) was clearly made because of the cumulative message which he wanted to draw out of each. We will consider this further below.

But how could John convince his readers that he had rightly interpreted the signs of Jesus? In the long run, of course, such conviction would be the work of the Holy Spirit (see 16:8–11). But one important factor here, especially for Jewish readers, was the Old Testament:

iii. *The Father writes his testimony in the Old Testament Scriptures.*

- "You diligently study the Scriptures because you think that by them you possess eternal life. These are the Scriptures that testify about me, yet you refuse to come to me to have life" (5:39–40).
- "If you believed Moses, you would believe me, for he wrote about me. But since you do not believe what he wrote, how are you going to believe what I say?" (5:46f.).

Supremely and finally, the Father's testimony to his Son is written in the Scriptures, as these two dramatic claims assert. In the development of these claims, John engages with the Old Testament throughout his Gospel, both by direct quotation (e.g. 2:17; 12:37–41; 19:36f.), and frequently by allusion to Old Testament texts or themes. His aim throughout is to show that only Jesus makes sense of the Old Testament.

For instance, the claim in 5:46 that "Moses wrote of me" leads into chapter 6, in which Moses' role as the Savior of Israel, the one who led them out of Egypt, is contrasted with what Jesus now offers. A crowd is on its way to Jerusalem for the Passover (6:4), the festival at which the Exodus from Egypt is commemorated. Jesus miraculously feeds them, just as Moses had done at the Exodus. Some of the crowd spot the similarity, and decide that Jesus could be the "prophet like Moses" (6:14). Jesus then addresses them (6:25–59). He tells them that:

- Moses did not feed Israel, but God did (6:32).
- The manna was purely physical food, and did nothing to save Israel from the awful enemy of sin and death (6:49). Moses

the supreme lawgiver could not meet the deepest needs of mankind.

- God has now provided food which will give "eternal life," and finally meet those needs—Jesus himself (6:35).
- The Old Testament itself recognizes the need for more than Moses gave; for the prophets look forward to a time when "they will all be taught by God" (6:45, from Isaiah 54:13). That time has now come!

John's challenge to his readers is the same as Jesus' to the Pharisees in 7:24, where the meaning of circumcision is under discussion: "Stop judging by mere appearances, and make a right judgment." If they will reassess their understanding of the Scriptures, they will see how Jesus fulfills them.

2. Surveying the Gospel

The structure of John's Gospel is complex, so any brief analysis is bound to be artificial. However we will follow John's own lead and focus our summary on the "signs."

a. Water into wine—a new order

The first chapter introduces Jesus as God's Word spoken in a new way. Previously, God spoke through prophets, like John the Baptist. But now his Word has "become flesh" (1:14). This means a whole new stage in his dealings with the world: "The law was given through Moses; grace and truth came through Jesus Christ" (1:17).

This "new order" is symbolized by the first sign, the changing of the water into wine (2:1–11). Jesus takes what Judaism offers as a means of purification (2:6) and transforms it into something that really meets need. This message is then carried forward: first Jesus cleanses the Temple, the focus of "old order" religion, and speaks of a new temple, his body (2:21). Then he tells Nicodemus, "Israel's teacher" (3:10), the repository of the profoundest learning available in Judaism, that he needs to be completely remade by the Spirit. And then the same message is communicated to the Samaritans, as Jesus offers them, through the woman, "a spring of water welling up to eternal life" (4:14), water altogether more important than that of Jacob's well.

b. Two healings—new life, new judgment

The two signs in 4:46–54 and 5:1–9 form a pair which are then interpreted through the great discourse in 5:19–47. In this discourse Jesus makes the boldest possible claim: that, as the Son, he exercises the privileges of God himself, in particular to give life (5:21) and to speak judgment (5:22). "Judgment" in this context does not mean just condemnation, but expresses the idea of royal decision and decree. As judge, Jesus the Son has the authority to decide life and death for all (5:25–30).

These two privileges have been "signified" in the two actions that precede the claim. Jesus speaks a life-giving word, "You may go. Your son will live" (4:50)—and the son lives. Then he speaks judgment to the lame man, not only in commanding him to rise, but also in telling him to carry his mat on the Sabbath (5:8–10), and in warning him, "Stop sinning or something worse may happen to you" (5:14).

c. Feeding the 5,000—Jesus the bread of life

Expounding his spiritual reenactment of the Exodus, Jesus claims three times to be "the bread of life" (6:35, 48, 51). When Jesus breaks the loaves and feeds the 5,000 (6:1–15—the only miracle recorded by all four evangelists), he is symbolizing the gift of his own flesh "for the life of the world" (6:51).

He is clearly referring to his cross. It is his torn flesh which is "real food," and his shed blood which is "real drink" (6:55). Only through his death is life available for us. Eating and drinking are a striking physical illustration of faith, that is, personal acceptance of Christ, absorption of his life into ourselves (6:57). Comparing 6:47 with 6:54, we see clearly that "believing" is equivalent to "eating and drinking."

If this discourse is historical, it can hardly have a direct reference to the Lord's Supper, which had not yet been instituted. However, many scholars believe that John wrote his Gospel against the background of the church's worship services, and that he himself interpreted this discourse as referring to the Holy Communion. It is certainly appropriate to feel that, when gathered to celebrate the Lord's Supper, we are especially able to exercise the faith of which this passage speaks.

d. Healing the blind man—Jesus the light of the world

If in chapter 6 Jesus claims to replace the festival of Passover, in chapters 7–10 he makes the same claim in relation to the greatest festival in the Jewish calendar, Tabernacles. The centerpiece of this section is the healing of the man born blind (chapter 9).

Here again a physical action symbolizes a spiritual truth. Twice in this section Jesus proclaims, "I am the light of the world" (8:12; 9:5). This is a reference to the famous light-ceremony which took place during Tabernacles, when great lamps were set up in the Temple, picturing the "pillar of fire" which Israel had to follow through the wilderness. But now Jesus calls out, "I am the light of the world. Whoever follows *me* will never walk in darkness, but will have the light of life" (8:12).

Since, after AD 70, Tabernacles could no longer be celebrated in the Temple, Jesus' claim addresses the need felt by many Jews at that time. They, too, like the formerly blind man who is thrown out of the synagogue (9:34), had lost their place of worship. But Jesus meets him, and restores his worship by giving him spiritual sight to match his physical sight. So, as he bows in worship of the Son of Man (9:35–38), he holds out hope and a message to all who need such restoration: worship the Son of Man, who is the light of the world, and you will truly celebrate Tabernacles!

e. Raising Lazarus—Jesus the resurrection and the life

The raising of Lazarus (chapter 11) is the last great public act of Jesus before his own death. John prepares his readers for it by the "Good Shepherd Discourse" in chapter 10. Here we learn that if Jesus is to reach out and minister to "sheep" like the blind man of chapter 9, then it will be at the cost of his own life. As the good shepherd, he lays down his life for the sheep (10:11, 14f.).

This self-giving by Jesus is dramatically enacted in chapter 11. He has escaped from violent hostility in Jerusalem and crossed the Jordan for safety (10:31, 39f.). Thomas knows full well that it will be suicidal to return to Jerusalem (11:16). But Jesus nonetheless returns because only he can save Lazarus. The raising of Lazarus is attached to the ringing claim, "I am the resurrection and the life" (11:25). But it is clear that Jesus can only be "the resurrection and the life" for Lazarus at the cost of his own life. And so we are not surprised when the Jewish Sanhedrin meets and decides that the raising of Lazarus is the last straw. If Jesus goes on like this the consequences will be incalculable. He must die (11:47–53).

So both Jesus' death and his resurrection are foreshadowed in chapters 10 and 11. Chapter 10 presents him as the good shepherd who dies for the sheep, chapter 11 as the resurrection who gives life to the dead. From this point the story takes its inevitable course. Jesus' departure looms (13:1). He withdraws into private with his disciples, and prepares them for a life in which enjoyment of his physical presence will be replaced by a spiritual union with him (chapters 14–16). Then follow the actual events of his arrest, death, and resurrection (chapters 18–21).

Through this compelling presentation John longs that his readers should come to share the faith, experience the life, and join the company of the followers of Jesus the Christ.

The Message of John's Letters

John's letters supplement his Gospel, although it is not clear whether they were written earlier or later. Scholarly opinions vary, but John's habit of addressing his readers as "dear children" (eight times), and of calling himself "the elder" (2 John 1; 3 John 1), suggests that he may be writing in old age. However, whatever the date, the message of the letters develops that of the Gospel. Clearly we cannot enjoy a gift unless we know that we possess it. Faith needs assurance. So if God means us to receive and enjoy eternal life (John 6:40), the knowledge that we have indeed received it is vital. John wrote his first letter, therefore, "to you who believe in the name of the Son of God so that you may know that you have eternal life" (1 John 5:13).

He was impelled to do this by the circumstances of his own church. If John was writing in old age, we may reasonably follow the evidence of Irenaeus and imagine him acting as an elder statesman in the church in Ephesus. Ephesus was a major city, and the cultural and economic center of a large surrounding region. It looks as though all three of John's letters were written to local congregations in the "greater Ephesian area," over which the elderly apostle exercised pastoral care and oversight.

The Ephesian church was evidently being disturbed by false teaching of a particularly dangerous kind. The heretical teachers are "antichrists" (1 John 2:18), "liars" (2:22), "deceivers" (2:26; 2 John 7), and "false prophets" (1 John 4:1). John wanted both to expose their hypocrisy and to confirm the faith of the true believers. The heresy appears to have been a kind of early Gnosticism, very similar to, if not identical with, that taught by one Cerinthus, who may well have been an opponent of John's in Ephesus.

There were three particular elements in this poisonous teaching.

1. Christological error

John charges the heretics with "having the Father, but denying the Son" (1 John 2:22f.; compare 2 John 9). Irenaeus helps us to understand this charge. They probably taught that Jesus of Nazareth was a mere man, the natural child of Joseph and Mary. Any idea of an incarnation was impossible to them, because they regarded matter as essentially evil. Upon this man, at his baptism, "the Spirit" or "the Christ" descended; only to leave him and fly back to heaven before the cross. So when John says that they "deny that Jesus is the Christ" (1 John 2:22), we should probably understand this to mean that they deny that Jesus and the Christ are one and same person. Later John describes their view as a denial of "Jesus Christ as coming in the flesh" (2 John 7; compare 1 John 4:2), and this seems to reflect the same distinction between "Jesus" and "the Christ."

For John, such rubbish is a denial of both the incarnation and the atonement. It robs Christ's person of divinity, his teaching of authority, and his death of efficacy. John affirms in the strongest possible terms that no one who rejects the Son can possess the Father (1 John 2:23f.). Jesus the Christ, the Son of God, is "he who came by water and blood" (1 John 5:6). This is an obscure phrase, but may well refer to his baptism and his cross, both of which, John declares in opposition to the heretical teaching, were experiences through which the divine-human Jesus of Nazareth passed.

2. Moral self-deception

The heretics were mistaken in ethics as well as in doctrine, and probably for the same basic reason. If matter is essentially evil, not only is an incarnation impossible, but the human body is a mere envelope for the spirit, and morality becomes a matter of indifference. Nothing which the body does can harm the spirit within. It is possible, they perhaps argued, to "be righteous" without "doing righteousness"—to be in a right relationship with God without corresponding righteousness of life.

This second error John strenuously denies.

- "The man who says, 'I know him,' but does not do what he commands is a liar" (1 John 2:4).
- "Dear children, do not let anyone lead you astray. He who does what is right is righteous, just as he is righteous" (1 John 3:7).
- "Do not imitate what is evil but what is good. Anyone who does what is good is from God. Anyone who does what is evil has not seen God" (3 John 11).
- "If we claim to be without sin, we deceive ourselves and the truth is not in us" (1 John 1:8).

So the child of God must "purify himself, just as he is pure" (1 John 3:3). John is uncompromising on this point:

> He who does what is sinful is of the devil, because the devil has been sinning from the beginning. The reason the Son of God appeared was to destroy the devil's work. No one who is born of God will continue to sin, because God's seed remains in him; he cannot go on sinning, because he has been born of God. (1 John 3:8–9)

John is not teaching the total impossibility of sinning, because he has stated in 2:1 that there is free forgiveness "if anybody does sin." He is teaching rather the total inappropriateness of sinning for someone brought to new birth by God. In this emphasis John is one with his Master: the Jesus who exposed the Samaritan woman's immoral life (John 4:16–18), told even righteous Nicodemus that he needed to be born again (3:1–15), warned the lame man to sin no more (5:14), told the Pharisees that they were mere slaves of sin (8:34), urged his disciples to keep his commandments (14:15, 21–24; 15:14), and prayed that the Father would keep and sanctify his own (17:17), this Jesus was the Holy One who required truth in the inward parts. "Dear children, keep yourselves from idols" (1 John 5:21) is John's last word to them.

3. Spiritual self-exaltation

The third aspect of the heretics' system which receives the apostle's condemnation was their superior attitude to others. They were religious snobs, claiming to have a special revelation of their own (4:1–3). They were the "spiritual" ones, the enlightened aristocracy, the religious elite. They despised the rest.

John flatly contradicts their claim. Writing to the whole church he says, "You have an anointing from the Holy One, and all of you know the truth. . . . [T]he anointing you received from him remains in you, and you do not need anyone to teach you" (1 John 2:20, 27). There is no esoteric revelation. The apostolic teaching—and the deep, inner conviction of its truth given by the Spirit—is the possession of the whole church.

Besides, members of the church must love one another. They are brothers and sisters. It was the Lord's last prayer that his disciples should be one (John 17:20–23). So no one can be "in the light" if he hates his brother (1 John 2:9–11). In fact, we should be ready to follow the example of Jesus and "lay down our lives for our brothers" (1 John 3:16). Such love is absolutely fundamental: "Whoever does not love does not know God, because God is love" (1 John 4:8).

But this love has been fundamentally denied by the heretics. By severing fellowship with the rest of the church, they have revealed their true colors: "They went out from us, but they did not really belong to us. For if they had belonged to us, they would have remained with us; but their going showed that none of them belonged to us" (1 John 2:19). They cannot claim to love God, and yet hate God's children (4:20f.).

John turns the threefold error of the heretics into a threefold test of authentic Christianity. As he undermines the false assurance of counterfeit Christians, so he buttresses the right assurance of real Christians. Like James, he draws a contrast between what people claim to be and what they really are. Often he uses a phrase such as "This is how we [or you] know . . .," to introduce tests of assurance, and these tests coincide with the errors of the heretics:

- "This is how you can recognize the Spirit of God: Every spirit that acknowledges that Jesus Christ has come in the flesh is from God" (4:2). This is the *Christological* test.
- "This is how we know who the children of God are and who the children of the devil are: Anyone who does not do what is right is not a child of God" (3:10). This is the *moral* test.
- "We know that we have passed from death to life, because we love our brothers" (3:14); "This is how we know that he lives in us: We know it by the Spirit he gave us" (3:24). This is the *spiritual* test.

John makes the same affirmations negatively:

- "Who is the liar? It is the man who denies that Jesus is the Christ" (2:22).
- "If we claim to have fellowship with him yet walk in the darkness, we lie" (1:6).
- "If anyone says, 'I love God,' yet hates his brother, he is a liar" (4:20).

These are the three proofs of genuine Christianity. John brings them all together at the beginning of his fifth chapter:

> Everyone who believes that Jesus is the Christ is born of God, and everyone who loves the father loves his child as well. This is how we know that we love the children of God: by loving God and carrying out his commands. (5:1f.)

Unless Christians are marked by right belief, godly obedience, and brotherly love, they are counterfeit. They cannot have been born again, for those who are "born of God" are those who believe (5:1) and obey (3:9) and love (4:7).

The language of John's letters is simple, but their message is profound. Martin Luther wrote of 1 John, "I have never read a book written in simpler words than this one, and yet the words are inexpressible." In them John distills the essence of a lifetime of discipleship, as he finally describes the truth, and the decision, upon which our whole existence hangs: "God has given us eternal life, and this life is in his Son. He who has the Son has life; he who does not have the Son of God does not have life" (5:11–12).

CHAPTER 5

Paul and His Message

I have been crucified with Christ and I no longer live, but Christ lives in me. The life I live in the body, I live by faith in the Son of God, who loved me and gave himself for me.

(Galatians 2:20)

The thirteen letters ascribed to Paul in our New Testament form almost exactly one quarter of the whole. Moreover, of all the New Testament writers, Paul might fairly lay claim to having been the most influential throughout the history of the church. For instance, it was a rediscovery of the theology of Paul which led to the Reformation in the sixteenth century, that theological revolution which prompted an upheaval within the Roman Catholic church and led to the birth of all the present-day Protestant churches.

Paul is also unique in that we know more about him than about any other New Testament writer. Luke devotes more than half of the book of Acts to telling the story of Paul's missionary ministry, and we also gather much about Paul from his letters.

Paul the Man

Paul was born in Tarsus, the principal city of Cilicia, on the southern coast of modern Turkey (Acts 9:11; 21:39; 22:3). He himself calls Tarsus "no ordinary city" in Acts 21:39. It was a town of considerable commercial importance, and possessed a university which ranked in fame with those of Athens and Alexandria. Paul probably never studied in the university because he received his main education in Jerusalem (Acts 22:3). But he clearly absorbed the Greek atmosphere and culture of Tarsus, and he spoke and wrote Greek with great fluency. He quotes from at least three Greek poets: Aratus (Acts 17:28), Menander (1 Corinthians 15:33), and Epimenides (Titus 1:12). Greek culture held few surprises for him, so his background equipped him well for his missionary career.

Paul enjoyed Roman citizenship by birth (Acts 22:28), which was an uncommon distinction. It suggests that his family was prominent in Tarsus, for in all likelihood his father or grandfather had received this official citizenship as a reward for services to the city. This may account for the fact that he had the Roman name "Paul" as well as the Hebrew "Saul" (Acts 13:9).

But "Saul" was the name he used as a young man. His family may have been thoroughly embedded in Greek culture, but for young Saul it was the religion of his fathers which won his whole heart and devotion. However, it was a particular version of that religion which captivated him. "I am a Pharisee!" was his passionate claim (Acts 23:6; compare Philippians 3:5).

Now Pharisaism was a distinct movement within Judaism, a movement which emphasized detailed obedience to the law, including scrupulous observance of the festivals and other rituals associated with the Temple in Jerusalem. For this reason, Pharisaism flourished in Judea, and few Pharisees were found elsewhere. But somehow Paul had come under the influence of this movement, and moved to Jerusalem at a young age to learn at the feet of one of the masters of Pharisaism, Gamaliel the First (Acts 22:3), the grandson of the famous Rabbi Hillel, to whom the whole movement looked as its founding father.

Young Saul of Tarsus threw himself eagerly into the task of

memorizing and observing the statutes and traditions of Phari-saism. He was, he says, "thoroughly trained in the law of our fa-thers" (Acts 22:3), and "was advancing in Judaism beyond many Jews of my own age and was extremely zealous for the traditions of my fathers" (Galatians 1:14). He went so far as to claim that he was "faultless" in his observance of the Law (Philippians 3:6). The final proof of his passion for the faith of his fathers was his savage persecution of the Christian church (Acts 9:1f.; 22:4f.; Galatians 1:13; Philippians 3:6; 1 Timothy 1:13).

Saul's conversion on the road to Damascus was sudden and dramatic. His zeal is shown by his readiness to undertake a long journey in order to root out all adherents of this foul "Way" (Acts 9:2). But suddenly a brilliant light flashed from heaven and blinded him; an unseen hand knocked him to the ground and "took hold of" him (Philippians 3:12); a voice called him by name; and he saw Jesus. There can be no doubt that it was a true objective "vision from heaven" (Acts 26:19) of the risen Christ. It was no hallucina-tion. Paul is quite clear in the matter. It was the last resurrection appearance of Jesus: "Last of all he appeared to me also, as to one abnormally born" (1 Corinthians 15:8). Three days later, he was preaching in the synagogues of Damascus "that Jesus is the Son of God" (Acts 9:20).

Some have suggested that the violence of Paul's opposition to the Christian faith was an attempt to stifle doubts which were already preparing him for this change of mind. What impression was left on Saul by the sight of Stephen, praying for his execution-ers as they stoned him to death, and committing his life into the hands of the "Lord Jesus" (Acts 7:59f.)? What were the "goads" against which Paul had been kicking (Acts 26:14)? Were they his uneasy feelings that these Christians were right, after all?

Similarly, some have suggested that Romans 7:7-9 gives us some insight into his state of mind at this time: "I would not have known what coveting really was if the law had not said, 'Do not covet.' But sin, seizing the opportunity afforded by the commandment, produced in me every kind of covetous desire. . . . Once I was alive apart from law; but when the commandment came, sin sprang to life and I died." Is he describing a period of conviction before his conversion when he realized that his obedience to the law was not as "faultless" as he had thought?

It is *possible* that Paul was afflicted with doubt in this way. But the argument in Romans 7 is complex, and it is not certain that he is describing his personal experience. Moreover, his own direct testimony gives no hints of such doubts. On the two occasions on which Paul describes his conversion in Acts, he pictures himself as unwavering in his conviction and ruthless in his zeal as a persecutor. Similarly in Galatians 1:13-16 and Philippians 3:4-12, the two occasions on which he writes about his conversion, he expresses no doubt about his commitment and pride as a "faultless" Pharisee. The experience on the Damascus road may have been a bolt from the blue.

Whether foreshadowed or not, Paul's conversion was the turning-point of his life. One scholar, Dr. Seyoon Kim, has emphasized the close connection between Paul's conversion experience and the gospel which he then spent his life proclaiming. At that moment of encounter with the risen Christ, Dr. Kim suggests, Paul not only became a Christian, but also received what he later calls "my gospel" (e.g. Romans 2:16) and the commission to preach it worldwide. This certainly fits with Paul's own testimony in Galatians 1:11-12: "I want you to know, brothers, that the gospel I preached is not something that man made up. I did not receive it from any man, nor was I taught it; rather, I received it by revelation from Jesus Christ." Here Paul literally writes, "by revelation from Jesus Christ," and is undoubtedly referring to the revelation of Jesus on the Damascus road.

We may explore the truth of this if we ask: What went through Paul's mind as he thought and prayed in the darkness for those three days until Ananias came to lay hands on him? The distinctive emphases of his letters help us to imagine his state of mind:

1. *His mind was changed about Jesus.* Though crucified, Jesus was the Messiah after all. Men had hanged him on a tree, but God had raised him from the dead. Paul had had no hesitation in addressing him as "Lord." He had known that he had experienced a vision from heaven, and that Jesus was addressing him from risen glory.

2. *His mind was changed about the Law.* The Law had led him to persecute the Messiah! How could this be? Particularly in his letters to the Galatians and the Romans, we see Paul answering the questions with which he must have immediately begun to wrestle. He questioned his whole lifestyle as a Pharisee, and the understanding of the Old Testament which went with it—until he was able to see how the Scriptures witness for Jesus, and not against him.

3. *His mind was changed about salvation.* This follows from the last point. Previously, Paul had believed that salvation was bound up with his obedience as a Pharisee. He could be assured of a place in the Kingdom of God because of his zeal for "the traditions of my fathers." But there could be no place in the Kingdom for someone who persecuted the Messiah! This was the greatest sin imaginable.

   Yet instead of judging and rejecting him, God had revealed his Son to him, and had commissioned him to a special ministry. How was this possible? Paul had *experienced* his doctrine of justification, the message which carried him boldly across Asia Minor, through Greece, and eventually to Rome: God had simply accepted him, and had forgiven his sin, not because Paul had meticulously offered the right sacrifices in the Temple, but because Jesus had sacrificed himself on his behalf.

4. *His mind was changed about the church.* "Why do you persecute *me*?" the risen Christ had asked. It is probably not fanciful to see the birth of Paul's understanding of the church in that question. There was such a close union between the Lord

and his church that to attack the one was to attack the other. Eventually Paul came to think of the church as "the body of Christ," united to Christ by the Holy Spirit who indwells and animates it. No wonder he felt such lifelong shame about his persecution of those Christians: he had hated them because they were filled and inspired by the Spirit to confess Jesus as Christ and Lord.

5. *His mind was changed about the Gentiles.* It is not clear exactly when Paul received his commission to be an apostle to the Gentiles. In one of the accounts of Paul's conversion, Ananias tells him that God has chosen him to "be his witness to all men of what you have seen and heard," and shortly afterwards Paul has a vision in the Temple in which God sends him to the Gentiles (Acts 22:15, 21). In the other two accounts, the risen Jesus himself, in the initial appearance on the Damascus road, commissions him to preach the gospel to the Gentiles (Acts 26:16–18).

There is no contradiction between these versions. In Galatians 1:15f. Paul writes about the moment "when God, who set me apart from birth and called me by his grace, was pleased to reveal his Son in me so that I might preach him among the Gentiles." The call was part of the conversion, for if God accepted and "justified" people freely, as he had just accepted Paul, then this was a gospel for all mankind. Jesus was a Messiah for the world, not solely for the Jews.

Previously, Saul the Pharisee had built his life on the sharpest possible distinction between Israel and the Gentiles. Gentiles could find salvation, but only with difficulty, and only if they accepted circumcision and took upon themselves "the yoke of the law." Essentially, they had to become Jews in order to be saved. But Saul had now learned two things. With horror, he learned that the Law (as he understood it) had led him astray. And with amazement, he learned that God had now accepted him freely and by "grace," regardless of his misuse of the Law. Putting these two things together meant abolishing the distinction between Israel and the Gentiles, because "there is only one God, who will justify the circumcised by faith and the uncircumcised through that same faith" (Romans 3:30).

All that was needed was the faith that welled in his own heart in response to his vision of Jesus. How could he refuse it? In fact, he did not want to kick against the goad!

Paul the Letter-Writer

Before we attempt to summarize Paul's message, it will be helpful to survey his career as a letter-writer, and the contents of his letters. Scholars dispute many of the dates and the order of the letters. In particular, many dispute Paul's authorship of 1 and 2 Timothy and Titus, the so-called "pastoral epistles," and thus also cast doubt on the further period of ministry which they seem to reflect. However, in the summary below we have assumed that Paul wrote them.

Many scholars have also tried to trace developments in Paul's thinking between the letters. It is certainly possible that such developments took place, but we need to remember, first, that Paul himself believed that he received the gospel ready-made on the Damascus road, as we have seen; second, that all the letters date from the second half of his ministry, not from the early, formative period; and, third, that his letters were all prompted by particular problems, so that their emphases were dictated primarily by the needs of his readers. It is not inappropriate, therefore, to put together a summary of Paul's thinking which draws on all his letters simultaneously.

The Message of Paul

In a nutshell, Paul's message is salvation by the grace of God in Christ. "Grace" is a key term in his thought. It occurs eighty-six times in his writings. For him "grace" has to be contrasted with "law" (see, e.g., Romans 6:15 and 5:20; Galatians 2:21). This was what he had experienced: he had pursued a lifestyle of "law," believing that God required meticulous observance of rules that covered every detail of life. But he then found that this had led him astray from God, and that God had stepped in and simply accepted him in Jesus. This was sheer "grace," undeserved love and forgiveness shown to a blasphemer and persecutor of the Christ.

For Paul God's grace is not just an attitude of God (regarding him with love), but also an action of God (grasping and delivering him through Christ). This action is seen in two events: in the gift of Christ, in whom "the grace of God that brings salvation has appeared to all men" (Titus 2:11), and in the gift of the Holy Spirit, through whom God's grace is made real and effective for each person. As Paul puts it in Titus 3:5-7, "He saved us through the washing of rebirth and renewal by the Holy Spirit, whom he poured out on us generously through Jesus Christ our Savior, so that, having been justified by his grace, we might become heirs having the hope of eternal life."

We may take four great theological expressions, used by Paul, to summarize this message of the grace of God:

1. Justification—God puts us right

This is the basic theme of the letters to the Galatians and the Romans. To be "justified" means to be acquitted, or cleared, either by a human court or by God the Judge of all mankind. It is an expression used in the Old Testament, where judges are commanded to "decide the case, acquitting ['justifying'] the innocent and condemning the guilty" (Deuteronomy 25:1). Similarly God says about himself, "I will not acquit ['justify'] the guilty" (Exodus 23:7).

Before his conversion, Paul felt no problem over this. As a Pharisee, he believed that it was never necessary to be guilty before God, because God had provided detailed instruction in the Law to preserve mankind from sin—including instruction about how to make atonement for the occasional sins that might occur. But now, as a Christian, he startles his readers by describing God as one "who justifies the wicked" (Romans 4:5). That had been his experience—but it seems to contradict the Old Testament. How is this possible?

Light is shed in Romans and Galatians. Paul refers to a verse from the Psalms which he had perhaps overlooked as a Pharisee: "Do not bring your servant into judgment, for no one living is righteous [literally 'justified'] before you" (Psalm 143:2, quoted in Romans 3:20 and Galatians 2:16). In Romans, this quotation forms the climax of a long section (Romans 1:18–3:20) in which Paul shows that all humankind, Jews and Gentiles alike, are "under sin" (Romans 3:9). His estimate of the power of the Law has sunk to rock-bottom! All the Law achieves is to make us "accountable to God" and "conscious of sin" (Romans 3:19, 20)—in fact, "under a curse" (Galatians 3:10). So if God is going to justify us, he *must* "justify the wicked": there is no alternative.

And it is possible, because of Jesus. In Galatians 2:17 Paul writes, ". . . we seek to be justified in Christ." This expression "in Christ" is very common in Paul's letters, and means to be united to Christ, joined inseparably to him. We will consider below exactly what this union is. "In Christ" the wicked may be justified—but not just because they are "joined inseparably" to the sinless Son of God, and thus covered by his sinlessness. Paul's thinking is more profound. He thinks of a kind of exchange between us and Jesus: "God made him who had no sin to be sin for us, so that in him we might become the righteousness of God" (2 Corinthians 5:21).

This is where the cross comes in. It was on the cross that Jesus was "made to be sin" for us. This phrase could be translated "made to be an offering for sin," and perhaps this is in Paul's mind. He puts it similarly in Galatians 3:13: "Christ redeemed us from the curse of the law by becoming a curse for us, for it is written: 'Cursed is everyone who is hung on a tree.'" He became sin for us, and became a curse for us, so that we might be delivered from both.

We ask Paul: How does Christ's death enable him to bear the curse for us, and become sin for us, in this way? He answers: Because death *is* the "curse of the law" and "the wages of sin" (Romans 6:23). Ultimately, death is separation from God caused by sin. This death Christ died for us. He died our death. If, then, we are united to Christ, it is as true to say: "I died in Christ" as it is to say: "He died for me." Since Christ died my death and I am in him, God sees me as if I had died myself. Having died and risen with Christ, the Law's demands are met, and I am set free. The following verses say it in Paul's own words:

- "I have been crucified with Christ and I no longer live, but Christ lives in me. The life I live in the body, I live by faith in the Son of God, who loved me and gave himself for me" (Galatians 2:20).
- "He was delivered over to death for our sins and was raised to life for our justification" (Romans 4:25).
- "Christ's love compels us, because we are convinced that one died for all, and therefore all died. And he died for all, that those who live should no longer live for themselves but for him who died for them and was raised again" (2 Corinthians 5:14f.).
- "The death he died, he died to sin once for all; but the life he lives, he lives to God. In the same way, count yourselves dead to sin but alive to God in Christ Jesus" (Romans 6:10f.).

Paul's doctrine of justification was attacked by some other Jewish Christians. In fact, he had to respond to three criticisms, all of them reflected in the argument of Romans:

a. If salvation is simply by grace through faith in Christ,
   then what is the purpose of the Law?

Many of Paul's fellow Jews reacted as he would have done before
his conversion. When he arrived in Jerusalem at the end of his
third missionary journey, he faced "thousands" of Jewish Christians who were deeply suspicious of him. As James described
them, "They have been informed that you teach all the Jews who
live among the Gentiles to turn away from Moses, telling them
not to circumcise their children or live according to our customs"
(Acts 21:21). There was more exaggeration than truth in this report. Paul was happy for Jews to continue to observe the Law
(Romans 14:3f.). But he certainly believed that keeping the Law
was not necessary for salvation—which was radical enough!

Paul particularly tackles this question in Romans 7:7–14 and
Galatians 3:19–29. He has already boldly asked, "Do we, then, nul-
lify the law by this faith?" and firmly replied, "Not at all! Rather,
we uphold the law" (Romans 3:31). He had different ways of justifying this claim, but in Galatians he uses two pictures which summarize them all: "Before this faith came, we were held prisoners
by the law, locked up until faith should be revealed. So the law
was put in charge to lead us to Christ that we might be justified
by faith" (Galatians 3:23f.).

Here he pictures the Law first as a guard, and then as a guide.
The Law could not provide salvation, but it could keep people
under protective custody until they could hear and respond to
the gospel. And it could guide people, leading them to Christ by
showing how he fulfills the expectations of the Old Testament
and provides exactly what the Law itself could not provide. As
Paul puts it in one of his sermons in Acts, "Through him everyone
who believes is justified from everything you could not be justified
from by the law of Moses" (Acts 13:39).

b. If salvation is simply by grace through faith, "what advantage, then, is there in being a Jew?" (Romans 3:1)

Paul seemed to undermine the special status of Israel as God's chosen people with whom he had made the "covenant," the commitment to be their God forever (e.g. Genesis 17:7).

Paul certainly believed that there was now one way of salvation for Jews and Gentiles alike, that of faith in Christ. As he puts it in Ephesians, Jesus has "destroyed the barrier, the dividing wall of hostility, by abolishing in his flesh the law with its commandments and regulations" (Ephesians 2:14f.). But does this mean that God has rescinded the promises that made Israel God's special people? Answering this question is one of Paul's main concerns in his letter to the Romans, because he, too, clearly felt that it was a problem.

In Romans 3:2f. Paul insists that there is great advantage in being a Jew, and that Israel's unbelief will not make God abandon his commitment to her. Then he returns to the issue in Romans 9–11, and devotes three demanding, and closely argued, chapters to it.

It is the essence of Paul's doctrine of justification by faith that there is now just one way of salvation for all—faith in Jesus Christ. So Gentiles do not need to become Jews in order to be saved. Rather, both Jews and Gentiles need to give up their previous religion and become Christians.

This horrified many Jewish Christians. They believed that, because of Israel's special covenant position, Gentiles must become Jews in order to be disciples of Israel's Messiah. Their charge was: Paul, you deny God's covenant with Israel by saying "there is no difference between Jew and Gentile—the same Lord is Lord of all and richly blesses all who call upon him" (Romans 10:12). Romans 9–11 is Paul's response to this charge. These fascinating chapters have become a great center of interest in recent scholarship.

Paul begins by affirming what his opponents thought that he denied. Yes, Israel is still the rightful bearer of the privileges God gave her (9:3-5), and God's word to her cannot fail (9:6). But Paul has some important things to say about the way in which God will keep his promises to Israel:

1. Keeping his word to Israel includes passing judgment on her for her sin and rebellion. It was never a blanket promise of salvation (9:27–29; 11:8–10).

2. Keeping his word to Israel does not mean a commitment to save every individual Jew. Simply being descended from Abraham does not automatically qualify Jews for heaven. God exercises a further choice (9:6–13). Yes, "all Israel will be saved" (11:26), but whether each Jew is included will depend on whether or not he or she responds to the gospel.

3. Keeping his word to Israel can run alongside an interest in saving the Gentiles. In fact, the two go together, firstly, because God promises in Israel's Scriptures to bless the Gentiles (9:25; 10:13, 20); and secondly, because one of Israel's founding documents, the famous Song of Moses in Deuteronomy 32, specifically warns Israel that if she falls into sin God will respond by pouring out blessings on other nations instead (10:19; 11:11–14). That is what has happened through Paul's ministry.

4. Keeping his word to Israel does not mean affirming Israel's understanding of her Law. She has great zeal for the Law, but actually fails to understand it. In particular, she fails to see that Christian faith is the fulfillment of the Law. This is because Christian believers, both Jews and Gentiles, display the transformation of heart for which the Law always longed, usually in vain (10:1–13).

5. And finally, keeping his word to Israel is something that God does over the whole sweep of human history. At times it might appear as though he has abandoned her. And that is how it appears at the moment, Paul says, because Israel has become "hardened in part" (11:25). But this "hardening," in God's scheme of things, allows the gospel to go out to the world—so that ultimately Israel will be drawn back into a wonderful climax in which "all men" will rejoice in God's mercy to them in Christ (11:25–32).

This brief summary cannot do justice to the complexity and

power of Paul's argument, which is one of the crowning glories of the New Testament.

c. If salvation is simply by grace through faith,
   then can we sin as we please?

Paul quotes this objection in Romans 6:1. Apparently he was even accused of teaching, "Let us do evil, that good may result" (Romans 3:8). Jewish Christians thought that his rejection of the Law inevitably meant the undermining of all morality. And indeed, some of Paul's Gentile converts were notoriously lax in their morals (e.g. 1 Corinthians 5:1; 6:15). What was Paul's reply? This third objection to his doctrine of justification by faith leads us into the next great theme in his theology:

2. Sanctification—God makes us holy

Justification is instantaneous. As soon as any sinner turns from his or her sin and commits himself or herself to Jesus Christ who died for them and rose again, God pronounces him or her "righteous." They have been "justified through faith" and have "peace with God through our Lord Jesus Christ" (Romans 5:1).

But sanctification is the process which then begins—by which the sinner is gradually transformed into the image of Christ (2 Corinthians 3:18). Each is impossible without the other, for as Paul puts it to the Philippians, "He who began a good work in you will carry it on to completion until the day of Christ Jesus" (Philippians 1:6). If God has truly justified someone, then he will also sanctify them.

So no believer can propose, "Shall we sin because we are not under law but under grace?" (Romans 6:15). Justification does not mean the rejection of the Law, but its injection—into the hearts of all who believe in Christ, in fulfillment of Old Testament expectation (see Ezekiel 36:26f.). If we are justified, then "God has poured out his love into our hearts by the Holy Spirit, whom he has given us" (Romans 5:5). The whole point about dying with Christ is that we should also rise with Christ to a whole new quality of life, never possible for those who simply trusted in the Law (Romans 6:4–7).

But this will not happen automatically, without activity on our part; we need to work at it. As Paul puts it vividly to the Philippians: "Therefore, my dear friends, . . . continue to work out your salvation with fear and trembling, for it is God who works in you to will and to act according to his good purpose" (Philippians 2:12f.). God is at work in us—but this does not mean sitting back and letting him do it all. We need to "work out our salvation with fear and trembling," almost as if it depended on us.

And so Paul's letters teem with practical instruction about Christian life and behavior. Several of them can be clearly divided into two, the first half relating to the Christian faith, and the second to the Christian life: for instance, Romans 1–11 and 12–16; Galatians 1–4 and 5–6; Ephesians 1–3 and 4–6; Colossians 1–2 and 3–4. Paul's prayers are particularly revealing. He longs that his converts should be filled with truth and love, with righteousness and patience, with joy and thankfulness (see especially Ephesians 1:15–23; 3:14–19; Philippians 1:3–11; Colossians 1:9–14).

Two further facets of Paul's teaching about sanctification need to be mentioned: *means* and *incentives.*

a. The means of sanctification

What hinders it? For Paul, the means match the hindrances:

i. *The Devil*—so we need "the full armor of God" (Ephesians 6:11). Paul believed that "our struggle is not against flesh and blood, but against the rulers, against the authorities, against the powers of this dark world and against the spiritual forces of evil in the heavenly realms" (Ephesians 6:12). He is probably not describing (as some suggest) a full hierarchy of evil powers, so that each location has its own personal demon against whom we must fight. But he is certainly underlining the power and the wickedness of these spiritual forces at war with us. We ignore them at our peril.

Thus we need the six-piece armor that God gives (Ephesians 6:14–17), and we will know that we are wearing it effectively when we "pray in the Spirit on all occasions with all kinds of prayers and requests" (Ephesians 6:18). The effective, victorious Christian is marked by a life of constant prayer.

ii. *The flesh*—and so we need to "live by the Spirit" (Galatians 5:16).

"The flesh" is an important expression for Paul. The New International Version usually translates it "sinful nature," for instance in Galatians 5:17: "The sinful nature desires what is contrary to the Spirit, and the Spirit what is contrary to the sinful nature. They are in conflict with each other, so that you do not do what you want." "The flesh" is the continuing presence of sin and death even in Christians. Sin and death no longer reign over us, but they are still present within us.

This means a battle within. "The flesh" must be fought, in the power of the Spirit. It is a matter of life and death: "If you live according to the sinful nature, you will die; but if by the Spirit you put to death the misdeeds of the body, you will live, because those who are led by the Spirit of God are sons of God" (Romans 8:13f.). If we are to produce the "fruit of the Spirit," rather than "the works of the flesh," then we must "crucify the sinful nature with its passions and desires," and "keep in step with the Spirit" (Galatians 5:24f.).

This is vital. Paul's deep worry about the Corinthians was that they were "fleshly" (NIV "worldly"), and not "spiritual" (1 Corinthians 3:1). It would be his urgent summons to the church of this century, also. More important than all mission strategies and education programmes, more far-reaching than every new initiative and venture, more urgent than every other need, is the call to holiness: to "live by the Spirit," so that we will not "gratify the desires of the sinful nature" (Galatians 5:16).

b. The incentives to sanctification

Paul seldom makes an exhortation to holiness without adding a motive. What are these incentives?

i. Sometimes it is *the example of Christ.* For instance, Paul urges us

- to humble ourselves just as Christ "made himself nothing" (Philippians 2:5–7)
- to "live a life of love, just as Christ loved us and gave himself up for us as a fragrant offering and sacrifice to God" (Ephesians 5:2)
- to "accept one another . . . just as Christ accepted you" (Romans 15:7).

ii. Sometimes it is *the presence of Christ:*

- "Submit to one another out of reverence for Christ" (Ephesians 5:21).
- "Let us purify ourselves from everything that contaminates body and spirit, perfecting holiness out of reverence for God" (2 Corinthians 7:1).

In both these verses "out of reverence for" is literally "in the fear of." In both cases, the motivation is loving dread of grieving him in whose presence we live. We find the same motivation in 1 Corinthians 11:29 (reverent participation in the Lord's Supper), and in Ephesians 4:29–31 (not grieving the Spirit by abusing those in whom he dwells).

iii. More often, it is *the work of Christ*, for us and in us, which motivates holiness. Here are three examples:

- We have died and risen with Christ; therefore "count yourselves dead to sin but alive to God in Christ Jesus" (Romans 6:11), and "set your hearts on things above, where Christ is seated at the right hand of God" (Colossians 3:1).
- We have "taken off" our "old self" and put on a "new self, which is being renewed in knowledge in the image of its Creator" (Colossians 3:9f.). Therefore we must put off anger and lying, and clothe ourselves "with compassion, kindness, humility, gentleness, and patience" (Colossians 3:12).
- Because his Spirit is in us, our bodies are "members of Christ himself" (1 Corinthians 6:15)—that is, we are Christ's *limbs,* his arms and legs. Therefore we must glorify God with our bodies, because "you are not your own" (1 Corinthians 6:19).

iv. Frequently, it is *the coming of Christ* which motivates holiness. Paul was always working and praying towards "that day" when the Lord Jesus would come again, and he longed that his converts should be ready:

- "He will keep you strong to the end, so that you will be blameless on the day of our Lord Jesus Christ" (1 Corinthians 1:8).
- "The night is nearly over; the day is almost here. So let us put aside the deeds of darkness and put on the armor of light" (Romans 13:12).
- "And this is my prayer: that your love may abound more and more in knowledge and depth of insight, so that you may be able to discern what is best and may be pure and blameless until the day of Christ, filled with the fruit of righteousness

that comes through Jesus Christ—to the glory and praise of God" (Philippians 1:9–11).

3. Edification—God builds up his church

Justification and sanctification seem at first sight to be concerned solely with God's work in the individual believer. But they have a vital community dimension, also. For instance, the "fruit of the Spirit" is composed of nine qualities, none of which can be practiced or expressed by an individual in isolation from others: "love, joy, peace, patience, kindness, goodness, faithfulness, gentleness, and self-control" (Galatians 5:22f.). They all pre-suppose relationships. Even "joy" cannot be expressed in isolation, "peace" includes the idea of living at peace with others, and "self-control" presupposes the temptations and challenges which so frequently arise within human society.

Justification certainly had a vital individual thrust for Paul. After all, this was how he had experienced it himself, facing the Lord alone on the Damascus road. But it had immediate community implications. The Lord who appeared to him identified himself with Paul's victims. And so, as soon as he had been baptized and had a meal, Paul "spent several days with the disciples in Damascus" (Acts 9:19). He had been converted into a new community.

And he quickly realized that "justification by faith" meant the creation of a new body, composed of all who belonged to Christ, whatever their differences of background or social position:

- "There is neither Jew nor Greek, slave nor free, male nor female, for you are all one in Christ Jesus" (Galatians 3:28)
- "Here there is no Greek or Jew, circumcised or uncircumcised, barbarian, Scythian, slave or free, but Christ is all, and is in all" (Colossians 3:11).

These two verses illustrate Paul's fundamental conception. The old religious, racial, social, even sexual, barriers have been broken down because of the union of the church with Christ. They are one "in" Christ, who is himself "in" all of them. What creates this union with Christ? Paul's answer is simple: the Holy Spirit. We are accustomed to thinking of the Spirit as indwelling each individual believer, and this is an important element in Paul's teaching. But he also thinks of the Spirit as indwelling the church as a whole. "Don't you know that you yourselves are God's temple and that God's Spirit lives in you?" (1 Corinthians 3:16). The Corinthians are not just a voluntary association of individual believers, but together are a temple inhabited by the Spirit of God himself.

We may explore this further. Paul calls the church "the body of Christ" (1 Corinthians 12:27; Ephesians 4:12) or "one body" in Christ (Romans 12:5). Entry into this body is by the Spirit: "For we were all baptized by one Spirit into one body—whether Jews or Greeks, slave or free—and we were all given the one Spirit to drink" (1 Corinthians 12:13). When Paul calls the Spirit "the Spirit *of* Christ" (Romans 8:9), the logical circle is complete. The Holy Spirit is the *Spirit* of Christ, inhabiting the *Body* of Christ, and bringing all in whom he dwells into spiritual union with each other, and with the risen and ascended Lord Jesus.

For Paul this body is not static: like the human body, it grows. When he writes of church growth, he does not usually have in mind increasing numbers, but developing intimacy: "Speaking the truth in love, we will in all things grow up into him who is the Head, that is, Christ. From him the whole body, joined and held together by every supporting ligament, grows and builds itself up in love, as each part does its work" (Ephesians 4:15f.). This growth is what Paul calls "edification" in 1 Corinthians 14, where he tackles the issue of speaking in tongues in the Corinthian church. How should this practice be regulated? The principle on which Paul bases his answer is that of edification: whatever builds the church up—enlarges its understanding, deepens its worship, strengthens its love—is to be encouraged. Whatever does not should drop away.

What are the practical means of edification? For Paul there are two:

a. Fellowship

The unity of the church is not to be created. It is to be preserved, for it already exists. Paul encourages the Ephesians, "Make every effort to keep the unity of the Spirit through the bond of peace" (Ephesians 4:3). This "unity of the Spirit" he also calls "the fellowship with the Spirit" (Philippians 2:1) or "the fellowship of the Holy Spirit" (2 Corinthians 13:14), using the Greek word *koinonia*. This word points to the fact that we all belong to each other, that we share together in the same Savior, and that we have a responsibility to care for each other and meet each other's needs:

- "It is right for me to feel this way about all of you, since I have you in my heart; for whether I am in chains or defending and confirming the gospel, all of you share in God's grace with me" (Philippians 1:7)
- "Is not the cup of thanksgiving for which we give thanks a *participation* in the blood of Christ? And is not the bread that we break a *participation* in the body of Christ? Because there is one loaf, we, who are many, are one body, for we all partake of the one loaf" (1 Corinthians 10:16f.). The Lord's Supper vividly expresses our *koinonia* with each other and with Christ.
- Paul writes of the eagerness of the Macedonian churches to contribute to the collection he is making for the poor churches in Judea: "They urgently pleaded with us for the privilege of sharing in this service to the saints" (2 Corinthians 8:4).
- "I pray that you may be active in *sharing* your faith, so that you will have a full understanding of every good thing we have in

Christ," says Paul to Philemon (Philemon 6) just before he tells Philemon to welcome back his runaway slave Onesimus "as a dear brother" (16). Their *koinonia* in Christ undermines their old master–slave relationship, and makes forgiveness essential.

b. Ministry

Paul describes the "edification" process in Ephesians 4:1–16. Central to it is Christ's gift of ministries to the church:

> It was he who gave some to be apostles, some to be prophets, some to be evangelists, and some to be pastors and teachers, to prepare God's people for works of service, so that the body of Christ may be built up until we all reach unity in the faith and in the knowledge of the Son of God and become mature, attaining to the whole measure of the fullness of Christ. (Ephesians 4:11–13)

It is vital to note here that the "officers" in the church do not undertake the "works of service." Rather, it is their role to prepare the rest of the church to undertake "works of service." When the church works together in this way, it is edified, that is, becomes more like Christ.

In 1 Corinthians 12 Paul describes the same process in a different way. He explores the picture of the church as a "body." Each part *belongs* to every other part, and contributes something unique to the whole. Each part *needs* every other part, and depends upon its unique contribution. And each part *suffers* with every other part, feeling the pain (or the joy) as if it were its own. Paul applies all these thoughts to the church. Every believer has a unique ministry, given by the Holy Spirit (1 Corinthians 12:7), on which the life and wholeness of the church depend.

This emphasis is not in conflict with belief in an ordained or appointed "ministry." Paul himself "appointed elders" (Acts 14:23), and gives much advice to Timothy and Titus about the qualifications for, and conduct of, the ministry of elders and deacons. But it is certainly in conflict with a sharply held distinction between "clergy" and "laity." Moreover, Paul would certainly encourage us to see that leadership in the church is not solitary, but plural. Under the superintendence of the Holy Spirit, some parts will contribute more than others to the guidance and direction of the body, but every part will contribute something.

The final, most important factor is love: the "most excellent way" (1 Corinthians 12:31), the cement between the bricks, the sap of the tree, the oil in the joints, the blood that keeps the life of Jesus flowing through the limbs of his church!

4. Glorification—God brings us home

Paul's teaching about the growth of the church suggests a goal towards which growth is directed. He holds out the prospect of becoming "mature, attaining to the whole measure of the fullness of Christ" (Ephesians 4:13). Here we meet a vital element in his theology, one which sets his gospel in sharp contrast to both the various pagan philosophies he knew from his youth in Tarsus, and to the materialism which is fast becoming a world culture in this century. The present is shaped by the future, the world has a definite destiny, time and history will end, and one day God will "be all in all" (1 Corinthians 15:28).

For Christians, this means that "we rejoice in the hope of the glory of God" (Romans 5:2)—that is, we look forward to entering the direct presence of God himself, finally and fully delivered from sin and death, and ready to enjoy perfectly the intimate family love of children united at last with their Father.

The Holy Spirit is crucial here also. He does not just produce his fruit in us (sanctification), and does not just create the fellowship that builds us up (edification), but also assures us of this final stage in the process, our glorification:

- "We ourselves, who have the firstfruits of the Spirit, groan inwardly as we wait eagerly for our adoption as sons, the redemption of our bodies" (Romans 8:23): here the Spirit is the "firstfruits" of the harvest, the part that allows us to see what the harvest is like and assures us that the rest is coming.
- "We do not wish to be unclothed but to be clothed with our heavenly dwelling, so that what is mortal may be swallowed up by life. Now it is God who has made us for this very purpose and has given us the Spirit as a deposit, guaranteeing what is to come" (2 Corinthians 5:4f.): here the Spirit is a "deposit" or first installment of the heavenly life that awaits us.
- "Having believed, you were marked in him with a seal, the promised Holy Spirit, who is a deposit guaranteeing our inheritance until the redemption of those who are God's possession" (Ephesians 1:13f.): here the Spirit is a "seal," God's mark of ownership setting us apart for the moment of "redemption."

There are three aspects to Paul's teaching about this future:

a. The return of Christ

According to the Lord's own word, we tell you that . . . the Lord himself will come down from heaven, with a loud command, with the voice of the archangel and with the trumpet call of God. (1 Thessalonians 4:15f.)

At this stage in his life Paul expected that he would be still alive when the Lord returned: "We who are still alive and are left will be caught up . . . to meet the Lord in the air" (1 Thessalonians

4:17). And some ten years later this still seems to have been his hope:

> Our citizenship is in heaven. And we eagerly await a Savior from there, the Lord Jesus Christ, who, by the power that enables him to bring everything under his control, will transform our lowly bodies so that they will be like his glorious body. (Philippians 3:20f.)

But even at the time of the Thessalonian letters, he expected certain events to precede the coming of the Lord:

> That day will not come until the rebellion occurs and the man of lawlessness is revealed. . . . (2 Thessalonians 2:3)

And so by the time of writing 2 Timothy, just before the end of his life, Paul became convinced that he would die before the Lord returned:

> The time has come for my departure. I have fought the good fight, I have finished the race, I have kept the faith. Now there is in store for me the crown of righteousness, which the Lord, the righteous Judge, will award to me on that day—and not only to me, but also to all who have longed for his appearing. (2 Timothy 4:6–8)

Some suggest that, with the passage of time, Paul modified his ideas about the date of Christ's return. But this is unlikely. In fact, he probably shows us how Christians in all ages should expect the return of Christ. We should "long for his appearing." We should live urgently in the light of it. And we should only decide on our deathbed that it will not occur in our lifetime!

b. The resurrection of the dead

Paul expected the resurrection to take place at the return of Christ: "The Lord himself will come down from heaven, with a loud command, with the voice of the archangel and with the trumpet call of God, and the dead in Christ will rise first" (1 Thessalonians 4:16). This will be the moment of judgment, when "we must all appear before the judgment seat of Christ, that each one may receive what is due him for the things done while in the body, whether good or bad" (2 Corinthians 5:10).

It will also be the moment at which we are transformed, and made fit for life in heaven. "The trumpet will sound, the dead will be raised imperishable, and we will be changed. For the perishable must clothe itself with the imperishable, and the mortal with immortality" (1 Corinthians 15:52f.). Paul is very careful as he describes this "clothing with immortality." The resurrection of the dead does not mean the resuscitation of corpses. He makes a comparison with the process of germination. Just as seeds lose their existence as they produce a plant, so our physical bodies will be dissolved—but God will treat them as seeds to produce a whole new "spiritual body" which is imperishable, glorious, and powerful (1 Corinthians 15:35–44).

There is nothing automatic about this process. It is the grace of God, raising us from the death which is our physical destiny to the life which is his spiritual gift. Then "we will be with the Lord forever" (1 Thessalonians 4:17), seeing him "face to face" (1 Corinthians 13:12).

In what state do the "dead in Christ" exist before the resurrection takes place? Paul says little about this, but his answer is contained in the question. They are "in Christ"—or "with Christ," as he puts it in Philippians 1:23, when contemplating the possibility of his own death. We need to know no more than this. "He died for us so that, whether we are awake or asleep, we may live together with him" (1 Thessalonians 5:10).

c. Judgment and restoration

Paul expected the judgment of God to fall upon the world at the
return of Christ. At the moment, God is restraining his judgment
in order to allow time and opportunity for repentance (Romans
2:4f.). But there will be a day "when his righteous judgment will
be revealed," and then "he will give to each person according to
what he has done" (Romans 2:5f.). Paul's words are somber:

> [When Christ comes,] he will punish those who do not know
> God and do not obey the gospel of our Lord Jesus. They will
> be punished with everlasting destruction and shut out from
> the presence of the Lord and from the majesty of his power on
> the day he comes to be glorified in his holy people. (2 Thessa-
> lonians 1:8-10)

The church today largely needs to recover this teaching and
the sense of urgency which it gave to Paul's ministry.

But the other side of this coin is the restoration of all things.
Paul had a cosmic vision of God's plan. He created "all things"
through Christ and for Christ (Colossians 1:16). He now sustains
"all things" harmoniously in Christ (Colossians 1:17). Finally he
plans "to bring all things in heaven and on earth together under
one head, even Christ" (Ephesians 1:10). So the coming of Christ
will not just mean salvation for those who are his, but liberation
for the whole universe:

> The creation waits in eager expectation for the sons of God to
> be revealed. For the creation . . . itself will be liberated from its
> bondage to decay and brought into the glorious freedom of the
> children of God. (Romans 8:19-21)

No less an outcome could follow from so great a work—the
work of the grace of God in Christ.

This is the gospel for which God laid hold of Paul that day on the Damascus road. Having had an experience of grace, he is given a theology of grace. "By the grace of God I am what I am" (1 Corinthians 15:10). Facing the many hardships, dangers and uncertainties of his ministry, he knew that God would always lead him "in triumphal procession" (2 Corinthians 2:14). For the same great purpose of grace which had placed him in Christ for acceptance, and was liberating him from the power of sin in the fellowship of the body of Christ, would surely preserve him to the end—and will preserve us also.

CHAPTER 6

The Letter to the Hebrews

But when this priest had offered for all time one sacrifice
for sins, he sat down at the right hand of God. Since that
time he waits for his enemies to be made his footstool, because by one sacrifice he has made perfect forever those
who are being made holy.

(Hebrews 10:12–14)

The great theme of the letter to the Hebrews is the finality of
Jesus Christ. He is God's last word to the world, and has fulfilled all the Old Testament expectations, so that there is nothing
more to follow. The author employs many Old Testament ideas
and passages in expounding this theme so that his argument can
be demanding for modern readers to follow. But his basic message
is clear: Jesus, through his eternal priesthood and unique sacrifice,
has brought us an "eternal salvation" (5:9). We "have come . . . to
Jesus the mediator of a new covenant" (12:22–24), which shall
never pass away. Christ has ushered in the "last days" (1:2) and
"the end of the ages" (9:26), so now we have only to await the
consummation, when he shall appear again for final salvation and
judgment (9:28).

As always, understanding the message depends on grasping
the historical situation it addressed. The letter is written to "the
Hebrews." This title is not original, but it is almost certainly ac-

curate, for the prominent use of the Old Testament suggests the Jewishness of both author and readers. Even though it does not begin like a letter, Hebrews ends like one, addressing a particular group known to the author (13:19, 23), quite possibly in Rome.

We learn that they had been persecuted when they became Christians (10:32–34), and had gained a reputation for sacrificial service (6:10). But now the author is deeply concerned about them. He calls them "lazy" and "slow to learn" (5:11; 6:12), and repeatedly urges them not to turn "away from the living God" (3:12), but to "go on to maturity" (6:1).

Some scholars explain this exhortation by the theory that this group of Jewish Christians was being tempted to give up their faith and revert to Judaism. Others think that the author is worried simply by what he sees as lack of growth, or slackness, in their discipleship. Either way, the remedy is plain: if they can receive a clear vision of Jesus, and the final supremacy of his priesthood, sacrifice, and covenant, then their faith and zeal will be rekindled.

Who was the author? The early church father Origen commented wryly, "God only knows." Many, both in the early church and later, have ascribed it to Paul. The English Puritan theologian John Owen, who wrote a seven-volume commentary on Hebrews, devoted an entire volume to proving Paul's authorship, about which he "entertained no more doubt on the subject than if it had the apostle's own superscription." His enthusiasm to prove this was no doubt fueled by the fact that the Reformer John Calvin had thought otherwise ("I indeed can adduce no reason to show that Paul was its author"), and had proposed either Luke or Clement (a late first-century Bishop of Rome). Certainly Hebrews 2:3–4 seems to exclude Paul, for the author there identifies himself as a second-generation Christian.

Luther perhaps made the best guess in suggesting Apollos. The description of him in Acts 18:24 as "a learned man, with a thorough knowledge of the Scriptures" fits the bill; and his Alexandrian origin might explain the links that scholars have found between Hebrews and some of the ideas of the Greek Judaism especially associated with Alexandria.

All we know for certain about the author is what we can gather from his letter. Even a casual reading makes it clear that he had a thorough grasp both of the Old Testament and of Jesus Christ, and that he was deeply concerned to bring the two together, and to show how neither can be understood without the other. But his treatment of the Old Testament is without parallel, because he looks at it *through Jesus,* allowing his understanding of the person and ministry of Christ to revolutionize the interpretation of the Scriptures which Judaism had taught him.

Similarly he shows a deep awareness of Jesus: a spiritual awareness, which sees in his incarnation (2:14), obedience (10:5–7), suffering (5:7–8), death (2:9), resurrection (13:20), ascension (4:14), glorification (1:3), and second coming (9:28), God's means of dealing with the sin and death which plague humanity. But he does not simply impose his understanding of Jesus on to the Old Testament. He allows the Old Testament to teach him how to understand the salvation which God has brought about through his Son.

This author, therefore, is supremely well equipped to help us understand the Old Testament: to show us, in fact, what the new wine has done to the old bottles.

We may summarize the message of Hebrews under four headings:

The Supremacy of Jesus

The author's great concern is to show that Jesus is greater than all others in God's eyes. He strikes this note in the beautiful preface at the start of the letter (1:1–4), where he proclaims Jesus as a revealer far greater than all others. For all his love of the Old Testament, he boldly calls it "fragmentary and varied" (New English Bible) in comparison with the revelation now given by God through his Son (1:1–2). His Son is not just a mouthpiece of God, as the prophets were. He is "the radiance of God's glory" (guaranteeing the community of his nature with the Father) and "the exact representation of his being" (guaranteeing the distinctness of his person from the Father). Heir of all things, agent of creation, upholder of the universe, purifier of sins, he now sits at the right hand of the Majesty on high (1:2–3). It is this exalted Son, unrivalled in the dignity of his person and work, in whom the final revelation has been given.

Following this bold introduction, the author sets out to expound the supremacy of Jesus in relation to the great figures of the Old Testament. In turn he proclaims him superior to the angels (1:4–2:18), to Moses (3:1–4:13), and to Aaron (4:14–10:39). Each of these is chosen because of what they represent in God's plan: the angels because they were commonly known as "sons of God" and the Law was given through them (2:2); Moses because he was the great "servant" (3:5) through whom God had brought Israel into being and given her the Law; and Aaron because he was the High Priest whose ministry mediated forgiveness of sin.

1. Jesus greater than the angels, 1:4–2:18

In order to prove that Jesus occupies a position higher than all other beings in heaven and earth, the author employs a chain of Old Testament quotations, mainly from the Psalms (1:5–14). The way he uses these psalms is well illustrated by the quotation from Psalm 8 in 2:5–9. This psalm declares that God has made man "a little lower than the angels" in order to crown him with glory and honour, and "put everything under his feet." This cannot refer to man now, argues the writer, because all things are not in subjection to him. Therefore it must refer to the Man Christ Jesus, for we do indeed see him "crowned with glory and honor" (2:9).

Taking this line of interpretation further, in the expression "lower than the angels" in Psalm 8, the author finds a reference to the incarnation. God plans to bring many other "sons" to glory also (2:10), and this he has accomplished by making Jesus our elder Brother (2:11), who shares our flesh and blood, and indeed our death, so that he might destroy the devil, who holds us enslaved to death (2:14). So, by becoming less than the angels, Jesus has become "the author of their salvation" for all others in that position (2:10). He was honored not in spite of, but because of, his sufferings!

2. Jesus greater than Moses, 3:1–4:13

In 3:1 the author urges us "to fix [our] thoughts on Jesus, the apostle and high priest whom we confess." The theme of Jesus as "high priest" has just appeared for the first time, in 2:17, where Jesus is described as "a merciful and faithful high priest in service to God." It is interesting to note that the theme of Jesus' faithfulness is now taken up in the comparison with Moses, while that of Jesus' mercy is picked up and developed in the next section, which is devoted to the comparison with Aaron (see 4:14–16).

Moses was "faithful in all God's house" (3:2), and so was Jesus. But Moses was just a part of the house, albeit a vital part—whereas Jesus represents the builder (3:3–4). Again, the faithfulness of Moses was that of a servant; the faithfulness of Jesus is that of a Son. Again, Moses' ministry was forward-looking; the benefits of Jesus' ministry may be enjoyed now (3:5–6).

This contrast leads the author into a long and heartfelt appeal. For if dreadful penalties fell upon those who rebelled in the days of Moses, we must not harden our hearts against Jesus, who is greater than Moses. "We also have had the gospel preached to us, just as they did" (4:2). If they did not enter God's rest because of their unbelief, we must "make every effort to enter that rest, so

that no one will fall by following their example of disobedience"
(4:11). The author feels deeply the warning given by the example
of the Exodus generation, who received so much from God and
lost it all, and does not shrink from telling his readers that they
stand in the same danger.

3. Jesus greater than Aaron, 4:14–10:39

Now we are approaching the heart of the argument. After an introductory paragraph, this long central section begins and ends with
powerful exhortations in which the author underlines his warning
(5:11–6:12; 10:19–39). In between fall two long passages in which
he considers first the person of Jesus the High Priest (6:13–7:28),
and then his ministry (8:1–10:18).

The introductory paragraph (4:14–5:10) contains the first
mention of an important figure who will feature largely in this
section of the letter. Melchizedek hardly appears in the Old Testament—only in Psalm 110:4, quoted in Hebrews 5:6, and in the
story in Genesis 14:17–24 to which Hebrews 7:1–10 refers. But our
author finds him a most significant figure, for two reasons. Firstly,
his very presence in the Old Testament, exercising a priesthood
so different from that of Aaron, shows that the Old Testament
itself was aware of the incompleteness and imperfection of the
priesthood of Aaron and his sons: "If perfection could have been
attained through the Levitical priesthood . . . why was there still
need for another priest to come—one in the order of Melchizedek,
and not in the order of Aaron?" (7:11).

Secondly, the actual person of Melchizedek, as revealed in the
two passages which describe him, prefigures the person of Jesus,
in several ways:

1. Melchizedek was a royal priest, a "king of Salem" (that is,
   Jerusalem), who was also "priest of God Most High" (7:1).

By applying several royal psalms to Jesus in his first chapter, the author has prepared us to think of Jesus as sitting on the throne of David, fulfilling the Old Testament expectation of a king who can also be called God (e.g. Hebrews 1:8). Now the author develops the priestly aspect of the ministry of the king of Jerusalem—and it is fascinating to note that David and his successors do indeed seem to have exercised a priesthood as part of their office (e.g. 2 Samuel 24:25; 1 Kings 9:25).

2. Melchizedek steps on to the scene in the Genesis story without any introduction. We read nothing of his birth or death or parentage or genealogy, and in this, concludes our author, he symbolizes the "indestructible life" of the Son of God (7:3, 16).

3. Aaron was descended from Levi, and Levi from Abraham. So when Melchizedek blessed Abraham, and Abraham gave Melchizedek a tithe, the "Levitical priesthood" was submitting itself to Melchizedek in the person of its ancestor. The Levites were supposed to collect a tithe from the rest of Israel, and then they were commanded to tithe their tithe and give it to God (Numbers 18:26). The author of Hebrews argues that this gift was prefigured in Genesis 14, underlining the status of Melchizedek as one to whom divine honors are due (7:4–10).

4. Melchizedek thus did not belong to the priestly house of Levi, and so prefigured Jesus who was a priest (like David) descended from the tribe of Judah (7:13–14).

5. Unlike the Levitical priests, Melchizedek was appointed by a divine oath, according to Psalm 110: "The Lord has sworn and will not change his mind: 'You are a priest forever'" (7:21). This oath did not apply to the Levitical priesthood, because they did not continue "forever": "death prevented them from continuing in office" (7:23). But, like Melchizedek, Jesus holds his priesthood permanently because he lives forever. Consequently, he is "able to save completely those who come to God through him, because he always lives to intercede for them" (7:25).

The author argues by finding something in the Old Testament which cannot be explained in Old Testament terms—in essence, the very existence of Melchizedek and his priesthood; then he explains it in New Testament terms as pointing ahead to Jesus.

In 8:1 our author passes to a new phase of his argument. "Every high priest is appointed to offer both gifts and sacrifices, and so it was necessary for this one also to have something to offer" (8:3). He moves from the person of the priest to the nature of his sacrifice—which will turn out to be just as unique.

The Sacrifice of Jesus

This new section of the letter has a "concentric" structure.

This structure reveals the author's care in composition—and also the main lines of his thought. He makes three contrasts here: between the earthly and heavenly "tabernacle" or "sanctuary" (the *place* of ministry), between the old and new covenants (the *basis* of ministry), and between the old and new sacrifices (the *function* of ministry). Whereas the old High Priest entered the Most Holy Place in the Tabernacle once a year, on the Day of Atonement, bearing sacrificial blood, Jesus has now entered the heavenly sanctuary, where God is, bearing his own blood, the evidence of a sacrifice that does not need to be repeated, and which does away with sin once and for all (9:26). The result is a whole "new covenant": that is, the relationship between God and his people has been placed on a wholly different footing. Throughout this passage the author draws on the ritual of the Day of Atonement (described in Leviticus 16), and seeks to show how, at point after point, Christ's perfect sacrifice has fulfilled the imperfect foreshadowing of the Day of Atonement.

Concentrating on the understanding of Jesus' death here, we may point to four ways in which Jesus overcomes the limitations of the "first covenant":

1. The sphere of the sacrifice

It is not ceremonial, but moral. The author lays some emphasis on this. The old sacrifices provided for the sanctification of the "ceremonially unclean"—literally, they sanctified "for the cleansing of the flesh" (9:13), as simply "external regulations applying until the time of the new order" (9:10). But what is needed is a sacrifice able to "clear the conscience of the worshiper" (9:9)—that is, to bring about real, personal, and inner transformation. The old sacrifices needed constantly to be repeated, because they never provided worshipers with release from the feeling that they were guilty for their sins (10:2).

But now "the blood of Christ" forms a sacrifice which can "cleanse our consciences from acts that lead to death, so that we may serve the living God!" (9:14). This is why the author is so concerned about his readers' failure to grow as Christians: they seem not to have entered as they should have into the full experience of new covenant forgiveness.

2. The nature of the sacrifice

It is not earthly, but heavenly. Jesus died on earth, but in fact he "offered himself unblemished to God through the eternal Spirit" (9:14). About this sacrifice Hebrews says several vital things:

- *It was perfect.* Whereas "it is impossible for the blood of bulls and goats to take away sins" (10:4), Jesus was truly "unblemished," and able to "do away with sin by the sacrifice of himself" (9:26).
- *It was spiritual.* "Through the eternal Spirit" (9:14) probably means that Jesus offered himself in perfect spiritual harmony with God, anointed by the Spirit for his travail with sin and death. This means that by his sacrifice he has been able to

"purify" the heavenly sanctuary (9:23), that is to say, he has made it possible for us sinners to draw near to God without defiling the sanctuary where he dwells.

- *It was vicarious.* This is the most basic point of all. Christ maintained such unblemished spiritual harmony with God, while passing through a full experience of temptation and trial, sin, and death, that he has been able to "take away the sins of many" (9:28). Hebrews does not reveal how precisely the death of Christ is effective in making him a "source of eternal salvation" (5:9) for others. But 9:28 clearly pictures his death as a vicarious sacrifice, bearing the sins of others, drawing on the prophecy of the Servant of the Lord in Isaiah 53 (see especially verse 11), and possibly also on the ritual of the "scapegoat" on the Day of Atonement. In the latter, the priest had to confess the sins of Israel, laying his hands on the head of the goat, and then the animal was banished into the desert, to "carry on itself all their sins" (Leviticus 16:22).

3. The uniqueness of the sacrifice

It is single, not repeated. The expression "once" or "once for all" is a favorite with our author, occurring no fewer than four times between 9:11 and 10:14, with reference to the death of Christ and its consequences. The contrast, of course, is between the one, unique, and unrepeatable sacrifice of Christ and the repeated sacrifices both of the annual Day of Atonement and of the daily Temple rituals. By their very repetition, our author maintains, they proclaim their own ineffectiveness.

4. The achievement of the sacrifice

It is permanent, not passing. Whereas the old sacrifices gave temporary, external ritual purity, the sacrifice of Jesus prepares us to follow him into the sanctuary itself. He is not just our representative but also our forerunner (6:20). Now we too may "draw near to God . . . having our hearts sprinkled to cleanse us from a guilty conscience and having our bodies washed with pure water" (10:22): here, dramatically, the author applies to "us" the language that is reserved for the ordination of the High Priest in Exodus 29:21 and Leviticus 16:4. Just as Aaron was prepared for his annual admission to the Most Holy Place, so we too have been prepared for entry, and stand on the threshold, waiting for the "Day" to dawn when we may follow "our great High Priest" through the veil (10:19–25).

The thought of Christ's achievement through his sacrifice introduces the third topic which plays a crucial role in the thought of Hebrews:

The New Covenant in Jesus

The quotation of Jeremiah 31:31–34 in Hebrews 8:8–12 is the longest single quotation from the Old Testament found in the New. It is the famous "new covenant" passage in which Jeremiah bewails the corruption of heart which has ruined Israel, and proclaims a gracious threefold promise that God will write his laws on the hearts and minds of his people, reveal himself to each one individually, and forgive their sins. This promise of inward holiness, personal knowledge, and full forgiveness has been fulfilled, our author believes, through the sacrifice of Jesus.

So Jesus is "the mediator of a new covenant" (9:15); and this new covenant is "superior" to the old one, for "it is founded on better promises" (8:6). It promises real transformation of heart.

The old covenant was simply ineffective: "If there had been nothing wrong with that first covenant, no place would have been sought for another. . . . By calling this covenant 'new,' he has made the first one obsolete; and what is obsolete and aging will soon disappear" (8:7, 13).

The author supports his case with three arguments: firstly, with a *human illustration.* The Greek and Hebrew words for a "covenant" can also mean a "will" or "testament." Thus, as a will takes effect only when the testator dies, so the New Testament came into force only when Jesus died (9:15–17).

Secondly, he uses a *biblical analogy.* He declares that as the first covenant is ratified by shedding blood, so the new covenant is inaugurated by the blood of Jesus, which is "the blood of the covenant" (9:18–21; 10:29; 13:20; compare Matthew 26:28).

And thirdly, he employs an *argument from experience.* "By one sacrifice he has made perfect for ever those who are being made holy" (10:14). Once forgiveness has actually been given and experienced, there is no need for any further sacrifice (10:17–18): the new covenant is in force.

This theme of the finality of the new covenant is the crucial point for the writer of Hebrews. He began his letter with the cry, "How shall we escape if we ignore such a great salvation?" (2:3). He feared that his readers were doing that—ignoring or (more literally) not caring about what God had done for the world through Christ. As Jewish Christians they may have been tempted to think that Jesus did not add much to their Judaism, after all. This the author resists passionately. Jesus is unique. God has spoken and acted finally in the person, work, and covenant of Jesus Christ.

There can be no question of other "priests" in a sacrificial sense, since through our great High Priest we enjoy direct access to God and need no other mediator. Our sacrifice is a "sacrifice of praise" (13:15), not a "sacrifice for sin" (10:18). The new covenant is the last covenant, and will never be superseded: it is an "eternal covenant" (13:20), which brings to God's people an "eternal salvation" (5:9), an "eternal redemption" (9:12), and an "eternal inheritance" (9:15).

The message of Hebrews is uncompromising. To a world and a church which are tempted to say that many paths lead to God, and that Christianity is simply one religion among many, the author of this letter issues a sharp rebuttal. To take that view is to deny what God has done for the world in Christ. At whatever cost—even to the shedding of their own blood (12:4)—the author urges his readers to hold on to the uniqueness and finality of Christ, who has gone through shame and death to the right hand of God. We need to hear him today.

The Discipline of Jesus

With "therefore, brothers" in 10:19, the author begins to draw the practical conclusions from his presentation of Christ. The section 10:19–39 looks back to and balances the exhortation in 5:11–6:12. Here we meet both a powerful encouragement and a sober warning: an encouragement to hold on to the faith (10:22), hope (10:23), and love (10:24) which should mark followers of Jesus, "the great priest over the house of God" (10:21), and a warning of the awful consequences for us if we treat Jesus lightly and "deliberately keep on sinning after we have received the knowledge of the truth" (10:26). There is only one sacrifice for sin: so if we despise that sacrifice, "no sacrifice for sins is left, but only a fearful expectation of judgment" (10:26–27). It was certainly the belief of this author that his readers could lose their salvation and fall under God's judgment.

His exhortation continues into the three magnificent closing chapters of his letter. These chapters appear to develop the threefold theme introduced in 10:22–24, as chapter 11 lays emphasis on faith, chapter 12 on hope, and chapter 13 on love.

Faith is "being sure of what we hope for and certain of what we do not see" (11:1): living by the unseen is inevitable for those who stand on the threshold of the sanctuary, waiting for the High Priest to reappear (9:28). So we are not to "shrink back" but to "believe and be saved" (10:39), like the heroes of the Old Testament who also had to live by faith because they "saw him who is invisible" (11:27). Those old-time heroes were men of hope as well as faith. Some promises of God they inherited in their lifetime by faith, but in another sense "none of them received what had been promised" (11:39). The earthly blessings they received simply symbolized the spiritual blessings they did not receive. These blessings they awaited in hope, that is, in joyful and confident expectation. By faith, therefore, they held on to God in the face of deep suffering.

We must do the same. "Surrounded by such a great cloud of witnesses" we also must "throw off everything that hinders and the sin that so easily entangles" and "run with perseverance the race marked out for us." We must "fix our eyes on Jesus, the author and perfecter of our faith." He too, like the heroes of Old Testament faith, "endured the cross" because of "the joy set before him," and so we should "consider him who endured," lest we "grow weary and lose heart" (12:1–3).

After this stirring exhortation chapter 12 powerfully develops the themes of discipline and perseverance in the light of the hope that inspires us: the hope of entering "the heavenly Jerusalem," and of finally coming to "Jesus the mediator of the new covenant" (12:22–24).

The last chapter touches briefly on various aspects of the "loving each other as brothers" (13:1) by which we are to live while waiting for that Day. We are to be hospitable to strangers (13:2), to remember prisoners (13:3), to honor marriage (13:4), to prefer contentment to covetousness (13:5), and to respect our Christian leaders (13:7–9, 17, 24). With the rest of God's worshiping people we are "bearing the disgrace" for Jesus' sake, joining him "outside the camp" where he suffered—that is, outside the norms and values of the world which seeks earthly security. For "here we do not have an enduring city, but we are looking for a city that is to come" (13:13–14).

In the meantime we are to fill our lives with praise to God (13:15), to do good and share our possessions with those in need (13:16), and to pray for one another (13:18–19), looking to God to equip us to do his will and to please him (13:20–21).

Hebrews challenges "the lazy" (5:11; 6:12), the lazy both in mind and in discipline. It challenges the mind by its stretching vision of Christ, the Son of God who is the heir of all things, yet learned obedience through suffering and won forgiveness as the great High Priest; and it challenges discipline by its powerful exhortation to walk together in his footsteps through suffering and death to the right hand of God.

CHAPTER 7

James and His Message

As the body without the spirit is dead, so faith without deeds is dead.

(James 2:26)

The letter of James is the first of the "general epistles," so called because it was not written to a specific church or person, but generally, as a circular addressed "to the twelve tribes scattered among the nations" (1:1). This appears to mean that it was written to all Jewish Christians everywhere. It is unique in the New Testament, written in a lively and polished Greek style and employing much imagery. Christians have long valued it for its emphasis on practical obedience, although Luther called it "an epistle of straw" because 2:14–26 seems to contradict Paul's teaching on justification by faith. We will consider this problem below.

James the Man

At least three men with the name "James" appear in the pages of the New Testament. Firstly, there is James, the son of Zebedee and brother of John, one of the Twelve. He was beheaded at the command of Herod Agrippa I (Acts 12:1–2), and so he cannot have been the author of this letter. Secondly, there was another member of the Twelve called James. He was the son of Alphaeus (e.g. Mark 3:18), and is probably also James "the Less" or "the Younger," who is mentioned, for instance, in Mark 15:40. Our knowledge of him is very scanty, and it is unlikely that so obscure a person would have written a letter for general circulation and introduced himself simply as "James, a servant of God and of the Lord Jesus Christ" (1:1) without further qualification or description.

So we are left, thirdly, with James, one of the brothers of the Lord Jesus (Matthew 13:55f.; Mark 6:3). It is possible that he was the eldest brother, since he heads the list, "James, Joseph, Simon, and Judas." He certainly became the most eminent member of the family, after the Lord himself. At least from the end of the second century onward, this letter was ascribed to him and quoted as Scripture, and he is by far the best candidate as author. How much do we know of him?

When the public ministry of Jesus began, James and his other brothers did not believe in him (John 7:5; compare Mark 3:21), quite possibly because he seemed to them to disregard some of the commandments of the sacred Law which they had been taught to love and revere. They evidently accompanied him at different times during his ministry, both in Galilee (John 2:12) and in Jerusalem (John 7:1–10), but they had not committed themselves to him.

It is remarkable, therefore, that during the ten days which elapsed between the ascension and Pentecost, the brothers of the Lord are specially mentioned by Luke as finding their place in the believing, praying company of expectant Christians (Acts 1:14). Perhaps, at least in the case of James, the clue is given by Paul, who includes in his catalogue of those who saw the risen Lord the statement "then he appeared to James" (1 Corinthians 15:7). No account of this interview has survived, but it serves to explain how James became a believer.

James appears rapidly to have won the confidence of the others, and within a very short time he is seen as the leader of the

Jerusalem church (Acts 12:17). Paul calls him an "apostle" and states that he saw him on his first visit to Jerusalem within three years of his conversion, when he stayed a fortnight with Peter (Galatians 1:18–19).

In Galatians 2:1–10 Paul describes a second visit to Jerusalem, when again he met James. We cannot be sure whether this is the visit described in Acts 11:30 or that in Acts 15:2, because on both occasions Paul traveled with Barnabas, as in Galatians 2:1. But the Acts 15 visit involved an important encounter between Paul and James, similar to that described in Galatians 2. There Paul explains that he and Barnabas went to consult the apostles over the issue of the circumcision of Gentile converts. Paul had not compelled his converts to be circumcised, but there was a strong Jewish Christian lobby which maintained, "Unless you are circumcised, according to the custom taught by Moses, you cannot be saved" (Acts 15:1). At the conclusion of this meeting, "James, Peter, and John . . . gave me and Barnabas the right hand of fellowship when they recognized the grace given to me. They agreed that we should go to the Gentiles, and they to the Jews" (Galatians 2:9).

This very issue was discussed at the meeting described in Acts 15. James took the chair at it, and through his wise deductions from Scripture and experience led the conference to the decision that circumcision was not necessary for Gentile converts (Acts 15:19). The letter then sent out expressed something of a compromise, however: Gentile converts were asked firmly "to abstain from food sacrificed to idols, from blood, from the meat of strangled animals, and from sexual immorality" (Acts 15:29). So while circumcision according to the Law was not required, submission to some of the cultural regulations of the Law was.

Before we accuse James of inconsistency, we would do well to ask why these particular regulations were chosen. Undoubtedly, the purpose of the request was to enable table-fellowship to take place between Gentile converts and Jewish Christians who were still scrupulous about the Old Testament food laws. Such table-fellowship—which would, of course, include celebrations of the Lord's Supper—was only possible if Gentile participants agreed to eat "kosher" food. This is entirely in accord with Paul's principle of limiting one's freedom for the sake of "weaker" consciences (see 1 Corinthians 8:4–13), and so does not point to inconsistency on James' part. Rather, he was anxious to enable his fellow Jewish Christians to accept these Gentile converts into one fellowship.

It is easy to see, however, how James might be misrepresented. In Galatians 2:11–21 Paul describes an incident in the church in Antioch before the Jerusalem meeting. "Certain men came from James," and caused even Peter to withdraw from table-fellowship with Gentiles, "because he was afraid of those who belonged to the circumcision group" (2:12). It looks as though James' and Peter's minor concession to the Law may have been taken by some as opposition to the basic principle on which Paul insisted—that of admitting Gentiles to full fellowship without requiring them to become Jews.

This same zeal for the law of Moses is seen in the only other passage in the book of Acts which features James—Acts 21:17–26. Years have passed and Paul has completed two further missionary journeys since the first. Hundreds of Gentiles have been converted and welcomed into the church; they have been baptized but not circumcised. Paul has now returned to Jerusalem. The day following his arrival he and his fellow missionaries call on James and tell him of God's work among the Gentiles. James rejoices, and glorifies God. But he adds a caution; he reminds Paul that there are also thousands of Jewish believers who are "zealous for the law" (verse 20). They are convinced that Paul teaches his Jewish converts to forsake Moses. So James suggests that Paul should go into the Temple and publicly perform the rites of purification required by the law of Moses, to prove his loyalty to the sacred law of God.

Paul readily consented, but a difference in emphasis between him and James is clear. James is revealed in Acts as a Jewish Christian believer, who was concerned that the acceptance of the new faith should not involve the complete abandonment of the old. The gospel of Jesus had fulfilled, but not abrogated, the law of Moses.

It is not surprising therefore that James earned the nickname "the Just." The fourth-century church historian Eusebius wrote: "The philosophy and godliness, which his life displayed to so eminent a degree, was the occasion of a universal belief in him as the most just of men." He goes on to quote Hegesippus, who lived toward the end of the second century and who said that James was a Nazirite. "He was in the habit of entering alone into the Temple, and was frequently found upon his knees begging forgiveness for the people, so that his knees became hard like those of a camel, in consequence of his constantly bending them in his worship of God, and asking forgiveness for the people. Because of his exceeding great justice he was called 'the Just' . . ."

According to the Jewish historian Josephus, James was later martyred in Jerusalem, in AD 62. The circumstances of his martyrdom are intriguing, and shed light both on his character and on his letter. Though held in high regard by the people of Jerusalem, James was clearly feared and hated by the priestly aristocracy which ruled the city. The High Priest, Ananus, a Sadducee, seized an opportunity to have James brought before the Sanhedrin, tried, and stoned. Josephus also tells us that in this period there was much social strife between the wealthy aristocracy, to which Ananus belonged, and the poorer sections of the population. When we read the fiery words with which James denounced the exploitation of the poor by the rich (e.g. James 5:1–6), it is easy to understand how he must have provoked the hatred of men like Ananus. The "justice" which people saw exemplified in James must have been like that of Amos, who also spoke out strongly in God's name against economic exploitation.

James' Letter

Such was the character of the man who contributed what is probably the earliest of the New Testament documents. Many commentators give the epistle a date not later than AD 50, and some believe it to have been written as early as AD 45. In deciding the date of the letter, the evidence of 2:14–26 plays an important role. Whether James intended it or not, this passage can easily be heard as an attack on Paul's doctrine of justification by faith. This is certainly how Luther understood it. But we saw above that James was happy to give Paul "the right hand of fellowship" (Galatians 2:9), even if his own ministry had a different emphasis. And so it is easier to imagine James writing 2:14–26 at an early date, before Paul's ministry among the Gentiles had really got under way, than at a later time, when his words would certainly have been taken as critical of Paul.

At this early date, many Jewish Christians were still worshiping members of local synagogues—as indeed James was, in Jerusalem. It is quite possible, therefore, that the "synagogue" (NIV "meeting") to which James refers in 2:2 was, literally, the synagogue in which Jewish Christians still worshiped alongside Jews not yet convinced of the Messiahship of Jesus. And so, even though James addressed Christians, and was uncompromising about his own commitment to Christ, it is also possible that he hoped his letter would be read by other Jews, and that he composed it partly with them in mind. This possibility is supported by the content of the letter, which is deeply Jewish as well as thoroughly Christian.

Features of James' Letter

1. Its emphasis on practical obedience

The chief characteristic of the letter, as we should expect from such a man as James, is its emphasis on the necessity of practical righteousness in the Christian life. The spirit of the letter is reminiscent of the Old Testament prophets. And alone among the New Testament authors, James makes prominent use of the theme of "wisdom" (3:13–18), and draws on some of the main themes of the Old Testament wisdom writings (especially Proverbs and Job).

James uses more than fifty imperatives in his five short chapters, and is fond of pithy sayings such as "Man's anger does not bring about the righteous life that God desires" (1:20) and "Friendship with the world is hatred toward God" (4:4). Throughout he employs vivid metaphors and picture-language, which make his teaching highly memorable and recall Jesus' use of parables.

It is James' practical emphasis which lies at the heart of the difficulty posed by 2:14–26. Some scholars still follow Luther in maintaining that this passage sharply contradicts Paul:

Paul: "We hold that a man is justified by faith, apart from works of law" (Romans 3:28, RSV).

James: "You see that a man is justified by works, and not by faith alone" (James 2:24, RSV).

And both Paul and James use the example of Abraham to illustrate these apparently opposite points (Romans 4:1–5; James 2:21–23).

But this is a difference in emphasis, not in message. And the reason is not far to seek. Each had a different set of false teachers in mind. Paul's opponents were the Jewish legalists, while James' were the Jewish aristocrats (like Ananus). The legalists' way of salvation was "works"—moral and ceremonial acts performed in obedience to the law. The aristocrats' way of salvation was "faith," that is, mere orthodoxy of belief, bare adherence to Judaism without any clear practical obedience.

To the legalists Paul argues that we are justified not by our own good works but through *faith* in Christ. To the aristocrats James argues that we are justified not by a barren orthodoxy (which even the demons possess—"and shudder," 2:19), but by *works,* especially care for the needy. Paul, however, is swift to add that the faith which saves issues inevitably in good works (Ephesians 2:8–10; Galatians 5:6), while James affirms that the works which save spring naturally from a true faith (2:15), and the absence of good works reveals the absence of true faith (2:17).

We are, in fact, saved neither by dead faith (James 2:17) nor by dead works (Hebrews 6:1; 9:14) but by a living faith which results in "love and good deeds" (Hebrews 10:24). We cannot be saved by works, yet neither can we be saved without works. The place of works is not to earn salvation but to evidence it, not to procure salvation, but to prove it. The reality of our faith is revealed in the quality of our life: and in this Paul and James wholeheartedly agree, pointing rightly to Abraham who trusted God's promises, and therefore obeyed God's command.

2. Its reliance on the teaching of Jesus

There is strong internal evidence that James was familiar with both the Sermon on the Mount and other discourses of Jesus, because of the many points at which he echoes Jesus' words. As one old commentator remarked, "If John has lain on the Savior's bosom, James has sat at his feet."

We may list at least the following points at which James' teaching echoes that of Jesus:

- The Christian who is called upon to suffer trial is "blessed": James 1:2; Matthew 5:10–12.

- God's purpose is that we may become perfect: James 1:4; Matthew 5:48.
- He gives generously to all who ask: James 1:5 and 4:2; Matthew 7:7–8, but . . .
- the Father only gives good gifts: James 1:17; Matthew 7:9–11, and then . . .
- only to those who have faith: James 1:6; Mark 11:22–24.
- Jesus' disciples must not only hear the word but do it: James 1:22–25; Matthew 7:21–27.
- They must beware of riches, because it is the poor who are heirs of the Kingdom: James 2:5; Matthew 5:3 and Luke 6:20.
- They must love their neighbors as themselves: James 2:8; Mark 12:31.
- They must keep even the least of the commandments, not offending in one single point: James 2:10; Matthew 5:19; and
- show mercy if they would receive mercy: James 2:13; Matthew 5:7 and 18:33–35.
- They must remember that it is the tree which determines the fruit: James 3:12; Matthew 7:15–20,
- and the peacemakers who are blessed: James 3:18; Matthew 5:9.
- No one can serve two masters. Each must choose between God and the world, and between God and money: James 4:4 and 4:13–15; Matthew 6:24.
- He who humbles himself will be exalted: James 4:6 and 10; Luke 18:14; compare James 1:9f. and Luke 1:52.
- Christians must not speak evil of one another or judge one another: James 4:12; Matthew 7:1.
- They must not indulge in ambitious, worldly planning to get gain: James 4:13–17; Luke 12:16–21, for . . .
- wealth does not last. Riches rot, garments become moth-eaten, and gold tarnishes like rust: James 5:1–3; Matthew 6:19–21.
- Therefore, woe to the rich! James 5:1; Luke 6:24 and 16:19–31.

- Let the believer wait patiently and be ready for the Lord's coming, for he is near, even at the gates: James 5:7–9; Luke 12:35–40 and Mark 13:29.
- Finally, Christians must not swear at all, by heaven or by earth or with any other oath. Their word must be reliable. Their yes must be yes and their no, no: James 5:12; Matthew 5:33–37.

James draws, above all, on the ethical teaching of Jesus. Because he was writing before any of our Gospels had been published, his letter bears ample testimony to the way in which the teaching of Jesus had become part of the marrow of the early church. At no point does James formally quote Jesus: he had soaked himself to such an extent in the teaching of his Lord that he automatically reflects it in his own.

3. Its sense of harmony between the Law and the gospel

This point follows from the last. Alongside this implicit dependence on the teaching of Jesus is an explicit dependence on "the royal law found in Scripture" (2:8). James seems to think especially of the moral, rather than of the ceremonial, law. But this moral law must be kept at every point: it is "the law that gives freedom," and by it we will be judged (2:12).

The gospel and the Law merge into each other for James. As Christians we have been brought to new birth by "the word of truth" (1:18), and this "word" must become a new principle of life within us, implanted into our hearts (1:21). Only so will we be able to escape the error of hearing the word and not doing it. If the word is implanted in us, we will be like "the man who looks intently into the perfect law that gives freedom, and continues to do this, not forgetting what he has heard, but doing it . . ." (1:25). Joined with the gospel, the law of Moses really becomes "the perfect law that gives freedom."

Above all, Christians must fulfill "the royal law" (2:8), the law governing the citizens of God's Kingdom (2:5): "Love your neighbor as yourself" (2:8). First promulgated through Moses (Leviticus 19:18), then sanctioned by Jesus (Mark 12:31), this law is still in force. If we show favoritism by exploiting the poor (2:9) we show that we are like the person with a mirror: we see that we need to wash, but we go away and do nothing. To know what is right and not to do it is sin (4:17)!

4. Its sense of the danger of wealth

This, too, is something which James shared with his Lord, as can be seen in four powerful passages. James teaches the impermanence of wealth (1:9–11) and God's abhorrence of discrimination against the poor (2:1–11). He then attacks business people who leave God's will out of their plans (4:13–17) and landowners who mercilessly exploit their workers (5:1–6). So sharp is his language that one writer, Pedrito Maynard-Reid, goes so far as to argue that for James it was impossible for the rich to be saved.

This is surely going too far, however, for in 1:10 James refers to "the brother who is rich." His message to this brother is that he should not boast about his high position, but about his lowly status! For, like Job, he will find that "he will pass away like a wild flower" before the sun. In the meantime, he has a responsibility to use his wealth for the poor (2:14–16).

Generally, however, James seems to have in mind people such as the High Priest Ananus, who eventually engineered his death: rich, Sadducean aristocrats who owned large estates and cared little for the well being of the landless poor who worked them. Like Zacchaeus, such a man would need to give up his wealth, if he wanted to be saved.

5. *The three pillars of Christian life*

Scholars have recognized that the last two verses of the first chapter, 1:26–27, contain a summary of James' message. In these verses he draws a contrast between true and false religion, and provides a yardstick by which to measure both. We may imagine ourselves to be religious, but unless our religion is marked by certain clear characteristics, we are deceiving ourselves and our religion is "worthless."

James then outlines the three characteristics of real religion, which he calls "pure and faultless." They are: to "keep a tight rein on the tongue," to "look after orphans and widows in their distress," and to "keep oneself from being polluted by the world." This is a penetrating analysis of the moral duty of humankind. It includes our threefold duty to ourselves, to our neighbor, and to God. Tongue-control is an index of self-control. The visitation of orphans and widows is an example of brotherly love. To keep oneself unpolluted by the world is the negative counterpart to giving God the worship due to his name.

In the rest of his letter James takes up and develops these three themes in turn, and in relation to each other: the tongue in chapter 3, care for the needy in chapter 2, and resistance to the world in chapters 4 and 5. We will briefly explore his teaching on these themes as we now attempt to summarize his message.

The Message of James

1. *Self-control*

Having urged his readers in his first chapter to be "quick to listen" but "slow to speak" (1:19), James enlarges on the dangerous influence of the tongue in the celebrated passage in chapter 3 (1–12). He adds image to image in vivid, descriptive pen-pictures, underlining the baneful influence of the tongue, out of all proportion to its size.

James thus regards *speech* as vitally important in the Christian life—a yardstick of the reality of our discipleship. But in itself, the tongue is not the source of temptation. Temptation arises from our inner desires, which can give birth to sin and then produce death (1:15). James tells us that any desire which is not at root love for God can potentially lead us astray in this way and must be resisted.

James is particularly concerned about the control of anger (see 1:19f.; 3:9; 3:14; 4:1–3), and about its opposite, namely speech which encourages peace (3:17f.). Such speech results from divinely given *wisdom*.

2. The royal law

The second element in "pure and faultless" religion is love. James' exposition of this theme has two characteristics:

Firstly, *love leads to action.* Pious benevolence is no substitute for practical kindness. It is no good sympathizing with orphans and widows; we must look after them (1:27). It is useless to say to a beggar, "Keep warm and well fed": we must give him food and clothing (2:15–16). Christian love is not sentiment but service, not affection but action.

Secondly, *love is impartial.* Love recognizes no distinctions and abhors "favoritism." James pictures for his readers a scene played out in synagogues everywhere in his day: the rich man arrives and occupies a privileged seat as if by right, while the shabbily dressed worshipers must sit on the floor. Such class distinctions are wholly inconsistent with the royal law. As J. B. Phillips paraphrases 2:1, "Don't ever attempt, my brothers, to combine snobbery with faith in our Lord Jesus Christ!"

3. Faithfulness towards God

The third element in "pure and faultless" religion is "to keep one-self from being polluted by the world" (1:27). Expressed positively, this means being faithful to God in the midst of all the temptations and pressures of the world. By "the world" he means materialistic, pagan society, with its simple message: if you don't have, get!

But that is not the Christian way, James tells us. The Christian way is that of Job, who was patient in suffering (5:10f.), and the way of Elijah, who put all his energies into prayer (5:16–18). God is "envious" towards us, yearning for our undivided love (4:5), longing to keep us from the spiritual adultery of which the prophets accused ancient Israel (4:4). And this is where money can be such a snare, for all of us. Whether poor or rich, we can set our desire on material things so that we become "doubleminded" (1:8; 4:8), unfaithful to the Lord.

Let Christians rather be "rich in faith" and rejoice that they are to "inherit the kingdom" (2:5). Let them find their wealth in God. Let them humble themselves before the Lord (4:10), submit themselves to God (4:7), be filled with prayers and praises (5:13–18), and be patient "until the Lord's coming" (5:7).

The Christian life, according to James "the Just," is thus essentially a life of practical holiness. It begins indeed with faith in our Lord Jesus Christ (2:1), but the Christian adds: "I will show you my faith by what I do" (2:18).

CHAPTER 8

Peter and His Message

But rejoice that you participate in the sufferings of Christ,
so that you may be overjoyed when his glory is revealed.
If you are insulted because of the name of Christ, you are
blessed, for the Spirit of glory and of God rests on you.

(1 Peter 4:13–4)

Paul tells us that the three preeminent Christian graces are
faith, hope, and love (1 Corinthians 13:13). If he is himself the
apostle of faith, and John is the apostle of love, then Peter is the
apostle of hope. No doubt this is an over-simplification.

The first letter of Peter has a wider message than this. As E. G.
Selwyn, a famous British commentator, puts it, 1 Peter is "a micro-
cosm of Christian faith and duty, the model of a pastoral charge,
composed of diverse materials and of many themes." Neverthe-
less, the chief emphasis of the letter is on our Christian hope, a
glorious and certain hope which enables us to endure suffering
with patience and even joy. Like our Master before us, we must
suffer before entering glory.

Peter the Author

The first letter of Peter has been accepted as authentic from the earliest days. It is quoted by Clement of Rome in his letter to the Corinthians, usually dated in AD 96, although Clement does not specifically name Peter as the author. But from the time of Irenaeus onward the letter is regularly quoted as Peter's, and it figures in the list compiled by Eusebius of New Testament works which are beyond dispute.

Its Petrine authorship, however, is often challenged, largely on account of its excellent Greek style which, it is argued, could hardly be supposed to have come from a rough Galilean fisherman. However, the fine literary qualities of the letter can best be explained by supposing that Silas, who is mentioned in 5:12, was more than a mere secretary. There Peter says that he wrote "with the help of Silas" (literally, "through Silas"), and it may well be that Silas had a share in the composition of the letter—perhaps filling it out from dictated notes.

Peter's authorship is further supported by a number of features in the letter which suggest his personal reminiscences. He had had a vivid experience of the "living hope" which comes gloriously "through the resurrection of Jesus Christ from the dead" (1 Peter 1:3); he had also been "a witness of Christ's sufferings" (5:1), remembering his beating (2:20f.) and his silence before his torturers (2:22f.); and he could never forget the Good Shepherd's threefold command to "take care of my sheep" (John 21:15–17; compare 1 Peter 5:2).

From the earliest time more serious doubts have surrounded the authorship of the second letter. It certainly purports to come from Peter's hand (1:1), and seems to refer to the first letter (3:1), but the style is more abrupt and complicated, and scholars have wondered whether in Peter's lifetime Paul's letters could have been regarded as "Scriptures" alongside the Old Testament (3:16).

These and other arguments are serious, but they are not conclusive. If Silas was responsible for the polished style of the first letter, then the rugged Greek of the second could be Peter's own. Also, full weight should be given to the author's claim to have been present at the transfiguration (1:16–18), to have received from the lips of Jesus a prophecy about his own death (1:13f.; compare John 21:18f.), and to have been acquainted with "our dear brother Paul" (3:15).

If the letter was not written by Peter, then these references were deliberately fictitious, inserted by the author in order to create an appearance of authenticity.

While the ancient world was open to such "pseudepigraphy," as it is called, there is evidence that the practice was not acceptable in the early church. Michael Green refers to the story, recorded by Tertullian, of what happened to the author of the second-century work *The Acts of Paul and Thecla*. This was not a heretical work, but the author was deposed from office as an elder because he put his writing out under Paul's name. In any case, "pseudepigraphy" would seem incompatible with the emphasis in the letter on godliness and truth (e.g. 1:5–7; 2:2f.). An extensive review of the evidence leads Michael Green to the conclusion that, "The case against the Epistle does not, in fact, appear by any means compelling. It cannot be shown conclusively that Peter was the author; but it has yet to be shown convincingly that he was not."

Peter the Man

Simon Peter is perhaps the most attractive of all the writers of the New Testament. He figures prominently in the Gospel narratives and in the early part of the Acts, and his obvious weaknesses, as well as his towering strengths, endear him to the Christian reader.

Like his brother Andrew, Simon was a fisherman. They were partners with that other pair of brothers, John and James, the sons of Zebedee (Luke 5:10). They came from Bethsaida, on the northern shore of the Sea of Galilee (John 1:44), but Simon later made his home in Capernaum (Mark 1:21, 29) on the lake's northwestern shore, where he lived with his wife, his mother-in-law, and Andrew (Mark 1:29–30; compare 1 Corinthians 9:5).

It is not difficult to imagine Simon's temperament in those early days. As a disciple, he was liable to burst out with strong expressions of feeling (e.g. John 13:6–9; Matthew 26:33), and naturally became the leader of the whole group. He is named first in every list of the apostles, and acted as their spokesman (e.g. Matthew 16:15f.). We can picture him as a young, hot-headed northerner with a turbulent disposition. It is all the more significant, therefore, that Jesus nicknamed him "The Rock." This impulsive youth would become the solid and stable foundation on which the church would be built (Matthew 16:18).

But there is more to be said. Simon was a Galilean, and Galilee was a notorious hotbed of revolutionary Messianic hopes. In Galilee, more than in Jerusalem, people clung to the prophecies which promised the reversal of Israel's fortunes and the establishment of God's Kingdom. They longed for the day when the Messiah would bring the Roman occupation of the land to an end. Hotheaded Simon probably shared these revolutionary longings. Temperament and environment combined to make him one of those Jews who were eagerly awaiting "the redemption of Jerusalem" (Luke 2:38), "the consolation of Israel" (Luke 2:25), and "the kingdom of God" (Mark 15:43).

It is not surprising, therefore, that when news reached them that a prophet had appeared in the wilderness of Judea, Simon and his friends left their fishing and went south to hear him. Undoubtedly John the Baptist attracted many who expected him to be a prophetic deliverer, leading an uprising against Rome. Fired by revolutionary zeal, Simon was baptized by John and became his disciple. But John pointed away from himself to another, as Simon discovered when his brother Andrew came to fetch him with the thrilling words: "We have found the Messiah!" (John 1:41)—meaning not John, but Jesus.

This was Simon's first introduction to the one who was to become the object of all his hopes. He accompanied him, heard him, watched him, and wondered at him. Gradually the spark of conviction grew in him, until at Caesarea Philippi, among the hills at the foot of Mount Hermon, it burst into flame with his great confession of faith: "You are the Christ, the Son of the living God!" (Matthew 16:16). His hope was realized. This was the supreme moment of his lifetime. The Messiah had come. Jesus accepted the title, told Simon that the Father had revealed this truth to him, forbad the disciples to tell anyone that he was the Christ (Matthew 16:20), and began at once to teach them "that he must go to Jerusalem and suffer many things . . . and be killed" (Matthew 16:21).

This proved a remarkably difficult lesson for Simon to learn. His first reaction to Jesus' prediction of suffering and death was horror and denial. The Messiah could not be killed. He had surely come to reign, not to die. So he blurted out, "Never, Lord! This shall never happen to you!" (Matthew 16:22). But Jesus' response was even more abrupt, in fact almost violent: "Get behind me, Satan! You are a stumbling block to me; you do not have in mind the things of God, but the things of men" (Matthew 16:23).

It was a *temptation* to Jesus to think that he might be a Messiah of the sort that Peter wanted—victorious, reigning, exalted. The disciple who had just been the recipient of the Father's revelation had become the object of the devil's deception. For Jesus had not come to drive the legions of Rome out of the Promised Land; he had come to die for the sins of the world. The way to his throne was up the steep hill of Calvary. He must suffer before he could enter into his glory; the price of his crown was a cross.

But Peter could not understand and would not revise his prejudices. Only a week later he saw Jesus transfigured, clothed in his real glory, and his prejudices must have been confirmed—even though he heard Jesus talking with Moses and Elijah about "his departure, which he was about to bring to fulfillment at Jerusalem" (Luke 9:31), and even though Jesus repeatedly spoke of his coming suffering and death (Mark 8:31; 9:31; 10:33f., 45).

So, when the time came, Peter tried to resist. In the upper room, he at first would not let his Lord do the work of a slave and wash his feet (John 13:6–8). In the garden of Gethsemane he resisted the arresting party: he drew his sword, lunged out in the darkness, and slashed off the ear of Malchus, the high priest's servant (John 18:10). He could not let the King be arrested without a fight! But he must have felt frustrated and puzzled by Jesus' response to his heroism: "Put your sword away! Shall I not drink the cup the Father has given me?" (John 18:11).

Perhaps doubts were arising in his heart as he followed Jesus "at a distance" (Mark 14:54) toward trial and almost certain death. Had he been mistaken? Was this not the Messiah after all? He had boasted that he would be prepared even to die for him (Mark 14:31), but how could he give his allegiance to a defeated King, rejected even by his own nation? The final test came, and he denied Jesus, not once but three times. And he went out into the night to weep bitterly, tears not just of remorse but of cruel disillusionment. No doubt he followed the crowds up to Golgotha. He saw the end. The hope he had nourished was extinguished. The Messiah was dead.

It is hard to imagine the two days of hell through which Simon Peter then passed. But it is not hard to feel with him the overwhelming excitement of Easter Day. He ran to the sepulcher with John (John 20:1–10). The tomb was empty. The body had gone. And then he met the Lord (1 Corinthians 15:5). We do not know what was said at this private interview. But we do know that Simon Peter was given "new birth into a living hope through the resurrection of Jesus Christ from the dead" (1 Peter 1:3). He felt literally like a man reborn.

We also know that on the evening of that first Easter Day the Lord appeared to the apostles in Jerusalem and repeated what he had said earlier on the road to Emmaus. "How foolish you are," he had said to the two disciples. "How slow of heart to believe all that the prophets have spoken! Did not the Christ have to suffer these things and then enter his glory?" Then we read that "beginning with Moses and all the Prophets, he explained to them what was said in all the Scriptures concerning himself" (Luke 24:25–27). So now in the upper room he likewise laid emphasis on the *fulfillment* of Scripture in his death and resurrection.

That Peter learned this lesson is clear from his sermons in the early chapters of Acts. "You killed him . . . but God raised him . . . and we are witnesses": this summarizes his message. He was no longer ashamed of the sufferings of the Christ, for although they were caused "with the help of wicked men," they were also part of "God's set purpose and fore knowledge" (Acts 2:23). He told the Sanhedrin: "This is how God fulfilled what he had foretold through all the prophets, saying that his Christ would suffer" (Acts 3:18). But now he has been raised and exalted to be "Prince and Savior," the source of forgiveness for all who repent and believe (Acts 5:31; compare 2:38; 3:19; 4:12; 10:43). Yes, one day this Prince will act to save his people and to judge the world (Acts 3:19–21; 10:42), but there is no need for his followers to draw swords. All they need to do is to wait—and bear witness.

So the impulsive apostle who first defended, and then denied, his Lord stood undaunted before the Sanhedrin, and submitted humbly to cross-examination. He was flogged and imprisoned. He slept the evening before expected execution (Acts 12:6). And if tradition is to be believed, he finally died his Master's death, being crucified in Rome during the persecution unleashed by the emperor Nero (compare John 21:18f.). Simon's old fiery, fighting spirit was replaced by Peter's new and living hope. Like his Master, he would come to glory through the cross.

It was—and still is—a hard lesson to learn. The temptation to deny the necessity of suffering is alluring to the church. It is much more attractive to believe in a Christ who delivers us *from* suffering, than *through* it. But Peter points us firmly to this second Christ. The first was his initial dream, shattered on that resurrection morning when death was destroyed by one who had borne it himself, and not just defeated it from a distance.

Peter's first readers needed to hear this message as much as we do.

Peter's Message

The Christians to whom Peter wrote, "scattered throughout" the five provinces of Asia Minor (1 Peter 1:1), were evidently threatened by persecution. This was probably not an official persecution, but it was severe enough to be called a "painful trial" (4:12, literally "testing by fire"), and it was widespread (5:9). Peter wrote to them from "Babylon" (5:13), which is probably a code-name for Rome: like ancient Babylon, Rome and her empire are now the center of worldly opposition to God.

Peter's readers would have known what he meant. Living in Asia Minor, many of them had experienced the pressures of the imperial cult, which was especially strong in that area. Scholars used to believe that the imperial cult was something imposed by Rome: that is, in order to reinforce loyalty, the Roman authorities set up temples to the goddess "Roma" and required people all over the empire to offer incense to the emperor.

But recently it has become clear that it was really a popular movement, though also encouraged by the authorities. In gratitude for the benefits of Roman rule, local populations financed the building of these temples, and set up festivals at which the emperor would be worshipped as a god. Naturally they would look with great suspicion on people who refused to join in. But Christians could not. At the risk of appearing subversive, they had to hold back. Peter encourages them:

You have spent enough time in the past doing what pagans choose to do—living in debauchery, lust, drunkenness, orgies, carousing and detestable idolatry. They think it strange that you do not plunge with them into the same flood of dissipation, and they heap abuse on you. But they will have to give account to him who is ready to judge the living and the dead. (1 Peter 4:3–5)

How should Christians behave in such circumstances? What is the Christian attitude to undeserved suffering? How can Christians cope with alienation from society around them? These are the practical questions which Peter tackles, particularly in his first letter. What are his answers?

1. The example of Jesus

Peter turns the attention of his readers away from themselves to Christ. Seven times in his first letter he uses the words "suffer" or "suffering" in reference to Christ (1:11; 2:21, 23; 3:18; 4:1, 13; 5:1). He appears to glory in what he once rejected. Following the example of Jesus, Christians too must suffer. He uses the same words "suffer" and "suffering" nine times with reference to Christians (2:19, 20; 3:14, 17; 4:1, 15f., 19; 5:9, 10). "To this you were called, because Christ suffered for you, leaving you an example, that you should follow in his steps," he writes (1 Peter 2:21).

The word translated "example" is unique in the Greek New Testament. It means a teacher's copybook alphabet, the basic letters which children had to trace in order to learn their shapes. Similarly, we must learn the ABCs of Christian discipleship following the pattern of the life of Jesus. These words are eloquent coming from the pen of Peter who had said: "Lord, I am ready to go with you to prison and to death" (Luke 22:33), but who in the event had only "followed at a distance" (Luke 22:54). Later, on the shore of Galilee, he had heard again the Master's call "follow me!" (John 21:19), and this call he passes on to his readers. "When they hurled their insults at him, he did not retaliate; when he suffered, he made no threats. Instead, he entrusted himself to him who judges justly" (1 Peter 2:23). They must do the same.

2. *The reason for Jesus' suffering*

But the question arises, *Why* did Jesus set this example? If Christians must suffer merely because they are followers of Jesus, and he suffered merely because the world hated him, then being a Christian is a poor and unattractive prospect. Peter points his readers to the glorious reason for the sufferings of Jesus, a reason which makes their suffering worthwhile.

Jesus' death was not a ghastly accident. He "died [or suffered] for sins once for all, the righteous for the unrighteous, to bring you to God" (1 Peter 3:18). The great object of his sufferings was atonement, the bridging of the gulf between sinners and God. "He himself bore our sins in his body on the tree, so that we might die to sins and live for righteousness" (2:24).

Here Peter's knowledge of the Scriptures pays dividends. The phrase "he bore our sins" recalls the Old Testament sin-offering and the ritual of the scapegoat on the Day of Atonement. It also recalls Isaiah chapter 53, the prophecy of the "Suffering Servant" who will die for the sins of others. Peter must have known that Jesus had applied this prophecy to himself and had interpreted his death in the light of its teaching (see e.g. Luke 22:37).

In addition to the Day of Atonement and Isaiah 53, Peter also uses the Passover rituals to understand and explain the death of Jesus. "You know that it was not with perishable things such as silver or gold that you were redeemed from the empty way of life handed down to you from your forefathers, but with the precious blood of Christ, *a lamb without blemish or defect*" (1 Peter 1:18f.).

Through the blood of the physically perfect Passover lamb, the Israelites were rescued from slavery in Egypt. Now, through the precious blood of the sinless Christ "sprinkled" on us (1:2), we have been redeemed from the worse slavery of an "empty way of life."

The purpose of Christ's sufferings is thus made clear. Only through those sufferings could he enter his glory, when God "raised him from the dead and glorified him" (1:21). Jesus establishes a death-to-life principle which Peter finds symbolized in the story of the flood (3:20f.). The water that destroyed the rest of the world was the means of salvation for Noah and his family, floating in the ark. So now baptism symbolizes death with Christ, the only death which leads to life. Joined to Christ, we can think of our sufferings as also his; and so Peter tells us not to be surprised if God calls us to endure a "painful trial" (4:12). "Rejoice that you participate in the sufferings of Christ, so that you may be overjoyed when his glory is revealed" (4:13). The death symbolized in our baptism becomes a daily principle of living, as we give our sufferings over to Christ and rejoice that, in him, "he who has suffered in his body is done with sin" (4:1). Salvation is on its way.

This is a message of great comfort and great challenge: comfort to those suffering already, challenge to those who shrink from it or deny it.

3. Being God's people

Right at the start Peter addresses his readers as "strangers in the world, scattered . . ." (1 Peter 1:1), and repeats this description twice (1:17; 2:11). That was their problem. They were alienated from the world, did not belong, and suffered the rejection meted out to all "strangers." But this alienation can be viewed from another angle and described by another name: election. What really makes them different is that God has chosen them to be his, and from this perspective they are not scattered, isolated, and rejected, but "a chosen people, a royal priesthood, a holy nation, a people belonging to God. . . . Once you were not a people, but now you are the people of God; once you had not received mercy, but now you have received mercy" (2:9f.). Peter takes some of the great Old Testament names for Israel (see e.g. Exodus 19:5–6), and applies them to his scattered readers. There could hardly be a more powerful description of the church.

Belonging to each other, they can support each other through the trials they face:

- "Now that you have purified yourselves by obeying the truth so that you have sincere love for your brothers, love one another deeply, from the heart" (1:22).
- "All of you, live in harmony with one another; be sympathetic, love as brothers, be compassionate and humble" (3:8).
- "Above all, love each other deeply, because love covers over a multitude of sins. Offer hospitality to one another without grumbling. Each one should use whatever gift he has received to serve others, faithfully administering God's grace in its various forms" (4:8–10).

So Christians need not be afraid. God is building a house, based upon Jesus the cornerstone, and all those who belong to him are like "living stones . . . being built into a spiritual house to be a holy priesthood, offering spiritual sacrifices acceptable to God through Jesus Christ" (2:5). Though scattered in the world, they are yet the temple of God, the place where he dwells. So if they suffer, they need not despair. They can confidently "commit themselves to their faithful Creator" (4:19).

4. *Living in hope*

Peter's fourth answer to coping with suffering is hope—the very quality which seems to be most difficult to maintain when suffering comes. But Peter's hope is not a vague, irrational sentiment, or a bulldog determination simply to "keep your chin up!" This hope is centered on Christ, and anchored to history. It is a "living hope," created by the resurrection of Christ (1:3), and to be realized at his return (1:7). When he is "revealed" (1:7), our final salvation will also be "revealed" (1:5). Meanwhile, we are "through faith shielded by God's power" (1:5), and until Christ is revealed to our sight we can believe in and love him who is invisible, and can be "filled with an inexpressible and glorious joy" (1:8). "Therefore," writes Peter, "prepare your minds for action; be self-controlled; set your hope fully on the grace to be given you when Jesus Christ is revealed" (1:13).

So this hope is secure. If we share Christ's sufferings (4:13), we shall certainly share his glory (5:1); and we can be sure that the sufferings we undergo are purifying our faith as fire purifies gold (1:7). Hope indeed! Present weakness merely points to future strength: "The God of all grace, who called you to his eternal glory in Christ, after you have suffered a little while, will himself restore you and make you strong, firm, and steadfast" (5:10).

This stress on God's future is one of the vital emphases of Peter's second letter, particularly of 2 Peter 3. Here he argues against "scoffers" (2 Peter 3:3) who doubt the reality of final judgment. He first insists that an End is really coming (3:3–7), and then explains its apparent delay (3:8–10): this is due to God's "patience," because he wants to allow the fullest opportunity for repentance before judgment falls. Finally Peter draws out the practical implications for Christians: "Since everything will be destroyed in this way, what kind of people ought you to be? You ought to live holy and godly lives as you look forward to the day of God and speed its coming" (3:11f.). The certainty of God's future judgment is the motivation for our present holiness.

This note of judgment is not lacking from the first letter, also: "It is time for judgment to begin with the family of God," Peter cries (4:17). He does not fear the judgment of God, because he knows that "salvation" is waiting for him through Christ (1:5). Yet we need to be ready, and this supplies Peter's fifth response to suffering:

5. Being holy, doing good

The exhortation in 1 Peter 1:13–16 is particularly important, forming Peter's first moral charge to his readers. Having urged them to have hope (13), Peter goes on, "As obedient children, do not conform to the evil desires you had when you lived in ignorance. But just as he who called you is holy, so be holy in all you do; for it is written: 'Be holy, because I am holy'" (14–16). Their separation from the world is to be signalled by a notable difference from the world, one which points to the character of God himself.

The exhortation to "do good" comes repeatedly in the central section of the letter:

- "Live such good lives among the pagans that, though they accuse you of doing wrong, they may see your good deeds and glorify God on the day he visits us" (2:12).
- "It is God's will that by doing good you should silence the ignorant talk of foolish men" (2:15).
- "If you suffer for doing good and you endure it, this is commendable before God" (2:20).
- Like Sarah, Christian women should "do what is right [literally, *good*] and . . . not give way to fear" (3:6).
- "Who is going to harm you if you are eager to do good?" (3:13). With this question Peter concludes a long quotation from Psalm 34, which includes the exhortation to "turn from evil and do good . . . seek peace and pursue it" (3:11).

So though they may be charged with being subversive towards Rome, believers must "submit [them]selves for the Lord's sake to every authority instituted among men: whether to the king, as the supreme authority, or to governors, who are sent by him to punish those who do wrong and to commend those who do right [literally, *good*]" (2:13f.). They may still be persecuted, but they will at least be making "every effort to add to [their] faith goodness" (2 Peter 1:5). Such an effort begins a golden chain along which goodness is strung next to knowledge, self-control, perseverance, godliness, concern, and love. The result is clear: "If you do these things, you will never fall, and you will receive a rich welcome into the eternal kingdom of our Lord and Savior Jesus Christ" (2 Peter 1:10f.).

So Peter's final prescription for suffering Christians calls them to resist being deflected from the active, obedient expression of their faith. Whatever you are going through, Peter says, don't stop doing good!

It remains merely to comment on a distinctive theme in Peter's second letter. He devotes most of the letter to warning his readers against "false teachers" who have introduced "destructive heresies" (2:1). This false teaching seems to have been a mixture of skepticism and moral laxity: a denial of the second coming of Christ and future judgment (3:3–13), accompanied by devotion to lives of sensual pleasure (2:13–22). The fiery zeal of Peter's early years crackles from his pen as he describes, in words of strong indignation, the shameless wickedness of these false teachers, and their fearful destiny (2:1–10).

He also indicates how his readers may continue in the truth without wavering, after he is dead (1:13–21). They will still have two sources of authoritative teaching: the written *apostolic* word (15) which was based not on myths which the apostles had invented but on history which they had witnessed (16–18), and the written *prophetic* word (19–21). The apostles of the New Testament were only confirming the prophets of the Old. These prophets "spoke from God" (that is, with his authority), not on their own impulse, but as they were irresistibly carried along by the inspiring Spirit (21).

Peter wants to preserve his readers from the final calamity, that of losing hold of the gospel which alone can give sure hope in a suffering world. "Therefore, dear friends, since you already know this, be on your guard so that you may not be carried away by the error of lawless men and fall from your secure position. But grow in the grace and knowledge of our Lord and Savior Jesus Christ. To him be glory both now and forever! Amen" (2 Peter 3:17f.). Peter's deep love for his Lord, and his ardent determination to live for him alone, shine through these closing words of his second letter.

CHAPTER 9

The Message of Revelation

The kingdom of the world has become the kingdom of our
Lord and of his Christ, and he will reign for ever and ever.

(Revelation 11:15)

R evelation is well-placed as the last book in the New Testament. It was probably one of the last to be written. More than
any other book, it points its readers forward to the future that God
has planned for the world and for the church. Its picture of Jesus
is a compelling summary of everything that the rest of the New
Testament writes about him. And, while most of the other New
Testament books were written to specific groups of Christians,
Revelation seems consciously to have been written for the whole
church, in all times and places. So, for all these reasons, it brings
the New Testament to a fitting, and most inspiring, conclusion.

Revelation has had a chequered history. It began well, because
from the middle of the second century Christians believed that the
"John" who wrote it (1:4, 9) was the apostle John. But by the third
century questions had arisen. It is so different from John's Gospel,
both in language and in content—could it really be by the same
author? Also, by this time various "fringe" groups had started to
use Revelation to support eccentric theories about God and the
world, a process which has continued unchecked ever since. So
orthodox Christians began to feel that Revelation was unsafe. It

was the only book of the New Testament on which John Calvin, the sixteenth-century Reformer, did not write a commentary (apart from 2 and 3 John). Martin Luther was open in his criticism: he relegated it to the sidelines, saying that "Christ is neither taught in it nor recognized."

Today, Revelation continues to attract attention from the academy and church alike. Inevitably, in our survey of the message of this book, we must give special attention to the principles of interpretation which are appropriate for it.

"John" the Author

The identity of the "John" who wrote Revelation is as unclear today as it was 1,800 years ago. We gather certain things about him from the book itself:

1. He records the angel's reference to "your brothers the prophets" which suggests that he is also a prophet (22:9) and his book is a "prophecy" (1:3; 22:10). This means that he was deeply conscious of his solemn calling to convey the word of God to his readers (22:18).

2. At the same time he wants to be known just as the "brother" of his readers, and as their "companion in the suffering and kingdom and patient endurance that are ours in Jesus" (1:9).

3. At the time of writing he is on the island of Patmos in the Aegean Sea, where he has been sent on account of his preaching and his testimony to Jesus (1:9).

4. His prophecy is addressed to the seven principal churches in the Roman province of Asia (1:11), on the mainland not far from Patmos (1:9). It is clear that he knows their local conditions (both geographical and spiritual), and that he can write to them with an authority which they will recognize.

5. He uses an extraordinary Greek style, which has puzzled read-

ers ever since. Some have concluded that Greek was not his first language, while others suggest that he deliberately breaks the rules of Greek grammar because he is describing things which surpass the capacities of human language.

6. He was deeply versed in the Old Testament Scriptures, which suggests that he was a Jew. In addition, he was clearly also at home in the "apocalyptic" tradition, for Revelation belongs to a type of prophecy often called "apocalyptic." This is illustrated in the Old Testament by Daniel and Zechariah, and several other Jewish "apocalypses" have survived from the intertestamental and New Testament periods. Revelation has much in common with these, but also differs from them notably.

We can gather no more than this from the book itself. At first sight all these points could fit with the traditional ascription of the book to John the apostle of Jesus and son of Zebedee. However, the fifth point is a difficulty. It was Dionysius, Bishop of Alexandria (AD 247–65), who first disputed this ascription, because of the differences both in language and in content between Revelation and the other writings ascribed to John: "It has scarcely a syllable in common with them!" And so he concluded: "I cannot readily agree that the author was the apostle, the son of Zebedee, the brother of James."

This led the early church historian Eusebius, who reported Dionysius' view, to refer to the view of Papias, Bishop of Smyrna around AD 125, that there were two leading figures called "John" in the early church: John the apostle, and another whom Papias called "John the elder." Eusebius suggested that this second John was the author of Revelation, and many modern scholars have adopted his suggestion.

There is more to be said, however. Differences there may be, but there are also marked similarities between John's Gospel and Revelation. For instance:

- These books alone in the New Testament call Jesus "the Word" (John 1:14; Revelation 19:13), and give prominence to the title "the Lamb" (John 1:29, 36; Revelation 5:6 etc.—twenty-eight times altogether).
- The theme of "testimony" is important in both (e.g. John 15:27; Revelation 12:17).
- In both books Jesus is the giver of "living water" and is the final answer to "hunger" and "thirst" (John 4:10; 6:35; Revelation 7:16f.).
- Both books predict persecution for the church (John 15:18–6:4; Revelation 3:10; 13:7), but ultimate union with God in his presence, bearing his "name" (John 17:11, 20–26; Revelation 22:3–5).
- "The temple" is a vital theme in both books—both the earthly Temple in Jerusalem, and its heavenly counterpart.

What should we make of this? Reviewing the evidence, Professor George Caird wrote, "It is possible to put up a case for common authorship, though the balance of probability is still against it." We probably have to be content with ignorance on the point. It seems likely that the "John" of Revelation was not the John of the Fourth Gospel, but also that there was some connection between them which produced these coincidences of thought and language.

In the long run, however, his precise identification is not important. More crucial are the qualities of mind and experience which were employed in writing the book. And three of these call for particular comment:

1. John was deeply familiar with the Old Testament Scriptures

He never formally quotes from them, but there are over 400 recognizable allusions to Old Testament texts, people, or events.

He alludes to all parts of the Old Testament, although he is most at home in the Psalms and the prophets, and among the prophets refers especially to Isaiah, Ezekiel, Daniel, and Zechariah.

In many cases it is just that he reuses the language of the Old Testament, perhaps sometimes unconsciously, but more important still, he draws on the great ideas and events of the Old Testament. The exodus of Israel from Egypt is frequently in his mind; so also is Israel's exile to Babylon and God's deliverance of Israel from it. The whole theme of God's covenant with Israel is crucial for him. Throughout the book we find references to the Temple, its furnishings and its worship. And deeply written into his mind and heart is the faith of the psalmist, who looked out over a Gentile world which did not know God and declared, "The Lord reigns" (e.g. Psalm 99:1).

But John does not merely reproduce Old Testament texts or ideas. He develops them, indeed creates something new out of them. This is because:

2. John was the recipient of prophetic revelation

It started when the inspiring Spirit laid hold of him on the Lord's day (1:10). A loud voice told him to write what he saw and send it to the seven churches of Asia (1:11). He turned and saw in the midst of seven golden lampstands "someone 'like a son of man'" (1:13). By using this phrase "son of man," John makes two things clear: he knew that it was Jesus whom he saw, and he knew that he was seeing him as Daniel had once seen him—in the vision described in Daniel 7:9–14.

Then, as he describes what he saw (1:12–16), John uses language drawn from several places in the Old Testament:

- His hair was like that of God himself (Daniel 7:9).
- His eyes and his belt were like those of the mighty angel who appeared to Daniel by the Tigris (Daniel 10:5-6).

- His voice was like the voice of God which Ezekiel heard (Ezekiel 1:24).
- His mouth was like that of the great "servant of the Lord," whose coming was revealed to Isaiah (Isaiah 49:2).
- His robes were like those of the High Priest (Leviticus 8:7), and he was standing beside a lampstand like the one in the Tabernacle where the High Priest ministered (Exodus 25:37).

Inspired by the Spirit, John weaves all these themes together as he describes his vision of the risen Christ in his glory. By doing this, John draws upon old themes in order to say something new: these different texts and themes are brought together, converging on Jesus Christ. As this process is repeated again and again through Revelation, Jesus becomes the key to understanding the whole Old Testament.

We might imagine the Old Testament as a film in black and white. Revelation is a "film about the making of the film" in glorious color. We are taken behind the scenes and shown the real action, introduced to the Director, and allowed to hear why the Director shot the film, and why he has now decided to carry on the story into a second film, with his Chief Executive as the star.

But Revelation does not just take us behind the scenes of the Old Testament. More than this, it takes us behind the scenes of the world itself. This "film about the making of the film" takes us right into the Director's office—that is, to the throne of God himself—and we watch him producing world history, in partnership with his Chief Executive. This is "apocalyptic," a word which literally means "drawing back the veil," so that we may see what usually remains hidden.

This leads us to the third quality John clearly possessed:

3. John had experienced the world's hatred of the church

He had been imprisoned on Patmos because of his witness. He knew that several of the seven churches to which he was commanded to write had already experienced persecution (2:3, 13), and that others would do so soon (2:10; 3:10).

This persecution seems to have been due largely to the Christians' refusal to join in the worship of the Roman emperor. The "imperial cult," as it is known, had been steadily growing. Julius Caesar had been declared divine posthumously in 29 BC, and there was a temple in his honor in Ephesus. Temples were erected to the next emperor, Augustus, while he was still alive, and also to his successor Tiberius. During the first century, the imperial cult gained momentum throughout the empire. Revelation is usually thought to have been written during the reign of Domitian (AD 81–96), who actually seems to have encouraged people to address him directly as "our Lord and God." This may be reflected in Revelation 11:17; 15:3; 16:7; 19:6: there is only one "Lord God," and it is not the emperor of Rome.

In Asia, the cult was very popular. Each of the seven cities except Thyatira had one or more temples dedicated to the current emperor or to the goddess "Roma." Local government was tied in with the cult. Annual festivals were held, marked not only by idolatry but sometimes by great immorality—and everyone would be expected to contribute to the cost of these, and to participate. As the processions passed by, people would sacrifice at small altars outside their homes. At this time Asia was peaceful and prosperous, and people attributed this thankfully to Roman rule.

When Christians stood back from all this, they appeared to be ungrateful and disloyal. The Nicolaitans seem to have given in to the pressure and counseled Christians to compromise. But for many the confession "Jesus is Lord" (1 Corinthians 12:3) meant that they could not sprinkle incense on the fire which burned before the emperor's statue and say, "Caesar is Lord." Was this why John was exiled on Patmos?

Beyond his knowledge of the immediate circumstances of the churches, John also knew what life on this globe was really like. Behind Asia's prosperous facade a much uglier picture lay hidden. The power of Rome rested upon military might, upon war, upon economic exploitation, upon the slave trade, upon the idolatrous worship of money and power, and—John saw it for himself—upon the dreadful authority of the dragon, Satan himself, and of the awful "beasts" to which he delegated power. To worship Rome was to worship the dragon himself, to receive his mark on the forehead (13:16f.). The Roman Empire might have looked prosperous and peaceful, but it was really a prostitute, sitting on the back of the dragon's beast (17:3), "drunk with the blood of the saints" (17:6), living in luxury at the expense of the world, and ready for destruction (chapter 18).

The "seals" in chapter 6 picture the reality of Roman rule. Imperial power (6:1f.), resting upon war (6:3f.), causing economic distress (6:5f.), spreading death (6:7f.) and the martyrdom of God's servants (6:9–11). John draws back the veil on all this horror, already experienced by many Christians, so that he might also reveal the wonderful victory won by God through his Christ, and promised by Christ to his servants. He had seen Jesus, risen, triumphant, glorious, invincible, holding the churches safely in his strong right hand. This was the vision needed by the persecuted church.

Interpreting Revelation

How should we understand this book? It has been the playground of cranks ever since it was written—and still is. Is there any way of assuring ourselves that we are reading the book in the way John intended?

There are essentially four approaches to the interpretation of this book. All efforts to unravel its meaning employ one of these approaches, or attempt to combine two or more. We will describe and assess them in turn, particularly in the light of the way in which John introduces his writing in the first chapter.

John describes his work in the very first verse: "The revelation of Jesus Christ, which God gave him to show his servants what must soon take place" (1:1). But we must ask, "Which servants?" and "What future is being revealed?"

- The *preterist* approach emphasizes the meaning of Revelation for its first readers, and questions any interpretation which does not keep them firmly in mind. They are the "servants" who will experience "what must soon take place."
- The *historicist* approach, on the other hand, views Revelation as a kind of almanac to world history, written in advance. This is the approach by which some, for instance, have identified the Pope as "the beast," or have found the European Union signified in the beast's ten horns (13:1).
- The *futurist* approach interprets "what must soon take place" even more radically. It maintains that Revelation is concerned only with the events of the End, the very last events in world history, including the coming of Christ and the final judgment.
- Very differently, the *timeless-symbolic* approach treats the book as a series of parables. What is important, this approach maintains, is the timeless truth conveyed by the powerful images of the book—images such as "the Lamb" and "the heavenly Jerusalem."

How are we to assess these rival approaches? In all probability they are not as mutually exclusive as they seem. But it is vital to listen to John himself, for his introduction gives us clear guidance on precisely this issue.

1. John defines the recipients of the revelation

God has given it to "his servants," mediated through John and the angel sent to him (1:1). In the greeting which follows, these "servants" are then named:

> John, To the seven churches in the province of Asia: Grace and peace to you from him who is, and who was, and who is to come, and from the seven spirits before his throne, and from Jesus Christ.... (1:4f.)

The book opens as a specific message, from all three persons of the Trinity, to the seven churches. So Revelation had a genuine historical context. John evidently exercised some kind of supervision over the churches in Ephesus and Smyrna, Pergamum and Thyatira, Sardis, Philadelphia, and Laodicea (1:11). He even lists them in the order in which they would be reached by a messenger traveling along the circular road which united them. And the particular needs of each church are addressed.

This definite historical context helps us in our assessment of these rival approaches. The *preterist* approach must have an important element of truth in it, while the strictly *futurist* school of interpretation cannot be correct. If the book's message wholly concerns the period immediately preceding the Lord's return, then it had no particular message for the churches for which John says he wrote it.

However, as we also saw above, there is evidence that a wider audience is also in view. This would suggest that the *preterist* school does not have a monopoly on correctness. The message may be directed primarily at the members of the seven churches, but it has relevance for all Christians everywhere. To illustrate this, we will look at one of John's most important visions, that of the dragon and the beasts.

One of the most horrifying pictures in Revelation is that of the woman sitting upon the beast with seven heads (17:1–6). As the vision develops, this woman is clearly identified as Rome. The seven heads of the beast "are seven hills on which the woman sits" (17:9). Rome was famous as the city built upon seven hills. The woman is actually called "Babylon the great" (17:5), but the first readers would have had no doubt of her true identity. So the whole vision was full of meaning for them. As they read John's words they saw the luxury of Rome, the trade on which she fed, her idolatry, and the exploitation essential to the economic system she controlled—and her coming downfall.

But if the woman is Rome, who or what is the beast on which Rome sits? This particular seven-headed beast has already appeared, in 13:1–10. John sees the beast rising out of the sea, the place of chaos, and the home of all forces hostile to God (13:1). Daniel had seen a vision of four beasts rising from the sea (Daniel 7:1–7), who turned out to represent four coming empires (Daniel 7:17). The single beast that John sees combines in one figure the four distinctive features of each of Daniel's beasts. These beast-empires had looked respectively like a lion, a bear, a leopard, and a vast dinosaur with ten horns (Daniel 7:4–7). John's beast repeats these features in reverse order: it has ten horns, and "resembled a leopard, but had feet like those of a bear and a mouth like that of a lion" (Revelation 13:2).

What should we make of this? To identify the beast simply as the Roman Empire on which the city of Rome sits will not do justice to John's imagery and this background in Daniel. A better interpretation lies at hand, one which gives Revelation a message for all believers in all times and places. The beast finds expression not in any single empire, but in all manifestations of imperial power which set themselves up against God and his people. Not all world powers persecute the church, of course. But many of them do—perhaps most of them, throughout history. Why is this? The answer is to hand: "The dragon gave the beast his power and his throne and great authority" (13:2). Ultimately, imperial power derives from Satan, because it rules the world without reference to its Creator and demands loyalty to itself.

John receives a matching vision of a second beast, this time "coming out of the earth" (13:11–18). The distinctive mark of the first beast was to make war (13:4), and to exercise "authority over every tribe, people, language, and nation" (13:7). The distinctive mark of this second beast is to compel loyalty to the first beast—in fact, to "make the earth and its inhabitants worship the first beast" (13:12). This the beast does by performing signs which "deceived the inhabitants of the earth" (13:14), so that they give their worship gladly.

John's original readers were surrounded by people who gladly participated in the imperial cult. They did so because they had swallowed Roman ideology about the *pax Romana,* and felt thankful to Rome for their prosperity, in ignorance of the realities of Roman rule so clearly seen by John. If the first beast represents oppressive imperial power, expressed in all manifestations of it, then this second beast could stand for the many ideologies by which empire sustains itself and compels loyalty. The imperial cult was sustained by a powerful priesthood which promoted it and wielded great influence, especially in Asia Minor. The propaganda issued by it was intense. Is this the second beast?

When the beasts are finally overthrown by Christ in Revelation 19, the second beast is pointedly called "the false prophet" (19:20). It deceives people into believing in salvation through secular power.

John therefore writes in a global way, expressing his message in terms which can be applied by Christians to their own situation, even if it is very different from that of his first readers. "His servants" (1:1) include all of us who "hear" (1:3) the words of this prophecy and seek to apply them to the world we inhabit.

So, while there is truth in the *preterist* view, the *timeless-symbolic* view must not be discounted. John provides the "revelation" which enables Christians in every age to see their world with new eyes.

2. John describes the character of the revelation

John calls his book "The revelation of Jesus Christ" (1:1). It is important to realize that this describes the content, as well as the source, of the book's message. The *historicist* approach, which discovers in the book a history of the world in code, tends to forget this essential principle. Quite apart from the variety of interpretations which the historicists have suggested, the chief objection to this method of interpretation is that it loses sight both of the church's need, and of the church's Lord. What a persecuted church needs is not a detailed forecast of future events which has to be laboriously deciphered, but a vision of Jesus Christ to cheer the faint and encourage the weary.

John's purpose is practical, not academic. He is not just a visionary; he is also a pastor. His desire is not to satisfy our curiosity about the future, but to stimulate our faithfulness in the present. He is told, it is true, "what must soon take place" (1:1), but the future which he foresees is wholly bound up with Jesus Christ, who is reigning now as "the ruler of the kings of the earth" (1:5), and who is returning soon (1:7). It is to him that John directs our attention, not just to the future. He is depicted in a variety of ways:

- First we see him among the lampstands, patrolling, investigating, encouraging the churches (1:12–2:1).
- Next, he is seen as the Lamb, close to the Father's throne, alone qualified to break the seals of the book of destiny (chapters 5–7).
- Then he is revealed as the Christ of God, who shares the victory and the rule of God himself over all opposing forces (11:15; 12:10).
- The scene changes again, and now he is the man-child to whom the sun-clothed woman gives birth and whom the dragon attempts to devour (12:1–6).

- Once again he is "the Lamb," but this time at the head of a singing army of the redeemed (14:1–5).
- Next he is the "son of man," the agent of God's final wrath and judgment (14:14–16).
- Matching this, he is portrayed as the warrior riding forth on a white horse at the head of the heavenly armies to judge and make war against his enemies (19:11–16).
- Finally, he is the husband for whom the church, his bride, descends from heaven adorned and perfected (21:1–9).

John saw these visions one after another, but this does not mean that they portray events on earth which happen in the same order. Each vision conveys some special truth about Christ which Christians in all ages can grasp and apply to themselves. Christ did not first spend a period of fellowship with the churches on earth, patrolling among the lampstands (2:1), and then depart for heaven to become the Lamb on the throne (5:6). Both visions are true for all time, and encouraging for all Christians.

Historical sequence plays a role at certain points, however. Several of the "sevens" noted throughout the book finish with a vision of final judgment or salvation. This is true for the sixth seal (6:12–17), the seventh trumpet (11:15–18), the sixth sign in heaven (14:14–20), the seventh bowl (16:17–21), and of course the concluding vision of the new Jerusalem (21:1–22:6). But in all these cases the preceding items in the series do not follow a step-by-step sequence leading up to the End. Each "seven" is like a series of photographs, viewing the same landscape from a different angle, each giving insight into a different facet of the world, its Lord and its future. This approach to Revelation was proposed over seventy-five years ago by the American scholar William Hendriksen, who gave it the name "progressive parallelism." His theory was that each of the sections of the book cover the whole of history, with a gradually increasing emphasis on the End, leading up to the grand climax in the final visions of judgment and salvation in chapters 20–22.

3. John indicates the method of the revelation

In the first verse of Revelation, John drops a further significant hint about the nature of his book. The word translated as "made it known" in the New International Version is literally "signified," the verb connected to the word "sign." This is the favorite term to describe the miracles of Jesus in John's Gospel, because they are all presented there as having an inner, spiritual meaning which is "signified" by the outward event.

Similarly, Revelation employs many signs or symbols which point beyond themselves to a deeper meaning which we, the readers, have to discern. More recently, scholars have emphasized that some truths can only be expressed through the use of symbol and metaphor, because these can give voice to ideas and thoughts at the very limits of our capacity to grasp and understand.

The imagery of the visions is very rich. It is derived from nature (e.g. horse, lamb, lion, locust, scorpion, eagle, tree, harvest, sea, rivers, earth, sky), from human life (e.g. commerce, warfare, idolatry, childbirth, prostitution, agriculture, medicine, government, building), and from the Old Testament (e.g. Babylon, Jerusalem, Jezebel, Egypt, Sodom, the Temple and its furniture, manna, the tree and the book, the water of life, Jesus as Lamb, Lion, and Root, etc.). Three principles should guide our interpretation of this imagery:

a. Much of it is used simply to give a heightened dramatic effect and does not possess an independent meaning in every detail

For instance, the precious stones decorating the walls of the heavenly Jerusalem (21:19) may not each symbolize something different. The same applies to the precious stones decorating the great prostitute (17:4; 18:16)!

b. The imagery is symbolical rather than pictorial, and is
   meant to be interpreted rather than visualized

We are not meant to imagine creatures "covered with eyes, in front
and in back" (4:6), but to remember their ceaseless vigilance. Nor
should we try to visualize a beast with ten horns, seven heads, and
one mouth (13:1–2), but should be impressed by the awful power
of the beast and its fearful blasphemy (13:5). Sometimes it is the
literal impossibility of the imagery which makes it powerful, as
in the case of the great multitude before the throne of God, who
have "washed their robes and made them white in the blood of
the Lamb" (7:14).

c. Even though some of the details are not "significant" by
   themselves, basically everything in the book should be
   regarded as symbolical, rather than literal

Some things are obviously literal, such as the references to the
Nicolaitans (2:6, 15) and the coming imprisonment of some of
the Christians in Smyrna (2:10). But if no literal reference is obvious, then a symbolical meaning should be sought—even when it
is clear that a "literal" feature of life in Asia Minor is in mind. For
instance, there was a pharmaceutical industry in Laodicea which
produced a famous eye ointment. But when Christ tells the La-
odiceans to "buy from me . . . salve to put on your eyes, so that you
can see" (3:18), the ointment symbolizes something else. Similarly,
the seven churches themselves are both literal and symbolic: they
are real churches, but they stand for the universal church of Christ.

It is the number "seven" which suggests what the churches
symbolize. In fact, the symbolism of numbers is one of the most
prominent features of the imagery of Revelation.

There is therefore truth in all four schools of interpretation.
The *symbolists* are right to insist that Revelation's imagery teaches

great truths about God, Christ, the church, the world, and the powers of evil which are vital for the church to learn in all times and places. The *preterists* are right to emphasize the relevance of these truths for its particular first-century setting and readers. The *historicists* are right to seek the relevance for the whole history of the world, not just that of the first century. And the *futurists* rightly underline its concern with the ultimate destiny of the world and the church.

A Pastoral Analysis

In a nutshell, what does the book teach the church of Christ? We may very briefly analyze its message as follows:

- **Chapters 1–3: The church's life in Christ.** This section is dominated by the vision of the risen, ruling Christ in chapter 1. His church may be weak, suffering, even complacent, but it rests in his hands and he ministers to its needs.
- **Chapters 4–7: The church's safety through Christ.** The visions in chapters 4–5 present God from an Old Testament (chapter 4), and then a New Testament (chapter 5), perspective. In spite of all the sufferings which are part and parcel of life in this world (chapter 6), the church is safe, "sealed" with a mark of ownership from God, who rules with unassailable power from the throne of the universe.
- **Chapters 8–11: The church's witness to Christ.** The trumpets announce God's warnings to a sinful and idolatrous world (9:20f.), while the church bears witness—symbolized first by John himself who is given a prophecy for the world (10:9–11), and then by the two witnesses, who bear faithful testimony in spite of dreadful opposition (chapter 11).
- **Chapters 12–14: The church's conflict for Christ.** What lies behind the world's opposition to the church? Here the veil

is drawn back, and we see the three real enemies, who have tried to destroy Christ himself and now try to destroy his people (12:17). Even though these enemies are "given power to make war against the saints and to conquer them" (13:7), yet, from another perspective, the church is safe, fed like Elijah in the wilderness (12:14), and gathered with the Lamb on Mount Zion (14:1–5).

- **Chapters 15–20: The church's vindication by Christ.** The vision of the church's enemies is followed by the vision of their destruction. The seals (chapters 6–7) describe what God *allows* in his world. The trumpets (chapters 8–11) describe how God *warns* his world. Now the bowls (chapter 16) describe how God *judges* his world. Then the destruction of Rome is pictured (chapter 18), followed by the overthrow of the three enemies, in the reverse order to that in which they were introduced in chapters 12–13.

- **Chapters 21–22: The church's union with Christ.** Having witnessed the final judgment of the world (chapters 15–20), John now sees the final destiny of the church. It is to be united with Christ in a "new creation" from which death and suffering have been banished, and which brings to a perfect fulfillment God's whole plan for the world.

The message of Revelation is powerful indeed. It centers on the vision of the Christ who shares his people's suffering and death and then shares the throne of God. It points us beyond the chaos and trauma of world history, and of our own lives, to our security in God's plan both for us and for the world. It takes evil seriously, but God even more so. It horrifies us with its stark portrayal of death and evil, then raises our spirits to heaven by putting on our lips words of the most wonderful praise. As we sing with the heavenly hosts, we know that the powers of evil have been defeated, and we are redeemed: "Salvation belongs to our God, who sits on the throne, and to the Lamb!" (7:10).

Subject Index

Scripture Index

NEW TESTAMENT

Langham Partnership is a global fellowship working in pursuit of the vision God entrusted to its founder John Stott—

> *to facilitate the growth of the church in maturity and Christ-likeness through raising the standards of biblical preaching and teaching.*

Our vision is to see churches in the majority world equipped for mission and growing to maturity in Christ through the ministry of pastors and leaders who believe, teach and live by the Word of God.

Our mission is to strengthen the ministry of the Word of God through:
- nurturing national movements for biblical preaching
- fostering the creation and distribution of evangelical literature
- enhancing evangelical theological education

especially in countries where churches are under-resourced.

Our ministry
Langham Preaching partners with national leaders to nurture indigenous biblical preaching movements for pastors and lay preachers all around the world. With the support of a team of trainers from many countries, a multi-level programme of seminars provides practical training, and is followed by a programme for training local facilitators. Local preachers' groups and national andregional networks ensure continuity and ongoing development, seeking to build vigorous movements committed to Bible exposition.

Langham Literature provides majority world preachers, scholars and seminary libraries with evangelical books and electronic resources through publishing and distribution, grants and discounts. The programme also fosters the creation of indigenous evangelical books in many languages, through writer's grants, strengthening local evangelical publishing houses, and investment in major regional literature projects, such as one volume Bible commentaries like *The Africa Bible Commentary* and *The South Asia Bible Commentary*.

Langham Scholars provides financial support for evangelical doctoral students from the majority world so that, when they return home, they may train pastors and other Christian leaders with sound, biblical and theological teaching. This programme equips those who equip others. Langham Scholars also works in partnership with majority world seminaries in strengthening evangelical theological education. A growing number of Langham Scholars study in high quality doctoral programmes in the majority world itself. As well as teaching the next generation of pastors, graduated Langham Scholars exercise significant influence through their writing and leadership.

To learn more about Langham Partnership and the work we do visit **langham.org**